CAUTION! USED

Philip Turner was born in Ch̶̶̶̶̶̶
Orpington in Kent and attend̶̶̶̶̶̶ ̶̶̶̶̶ood
School in Bromley. In 1980 he studied at the
University of East Anglia and after postgraduate
research trained and worked briefly as a land
surveyor.

He runs his own full-time vehicle-inspection
company and has contributed articles to a variety
of publications including *Buying Cars Magazine,*
Auto Express, Car Choice and the *Kent Messenger*
Group.

He has travelled extensively throughout the USA
and lived for a year in the Midwest – he is also
a frequent visitor to Russia. Philip Turner is
married and lives in Kent.

PHILIP D. TURNER

CAUTION! USED CARS

A SIGNET BOOK

For Lydia and Mikhail

SIGNET

Published by the Penguin Group
Penguin Books Ltd, 27 Wrights Lane, London W8 5TZ, England
Penguin Books USA Inc., 375 Hudson Street, New York, New York 10014, USA
Penguin Books Australia Ltd, Ringwood, Victoria, Australia
Penguin Books Canada Ltd, 10 Alcorn Avenue, Toronto, Ontario, Canada M4V 3B2
Penguin Books (NZ) Ltd, 182–190 Wairau Road, Auckland 10, New Zealand

Penguin Books Ltd, Registered Offices: Harmondsworth, Middlesex, England

First published by The Self Publishing Association Ltd
in conjunction with Philip D. Turner 1991
Published in Signet 1994
10 9 8 7 6 5 4 3 2 1

Filmset by Datix International Limited, Bungay, Suffolk
Printed in England by Clays Ltd, St Ives plc
Set in 11/13 pt Monophoto Plantin

Contents

List of Figures

Author's Note

It is important to stress that a book of this nature has not been without its preparation difficulties: the main ones being that the multitude of factors relating to a car's overall condition (be they structural, mechanical, electrical or otherwise) cannot always be dealt with coherently or in a convenient, straightforward fashion. For this reason there may be cross-referencing to – and possibly some repetition of – topics in other sections where considered appropriate.

Also, this book does not set out to cover every examinable detail of a car – there are simply too many of them with too many minor variations on vehicle design to make this practicable. Therefore, you would be wise to heed any other valuable advice from as many other relevant sources to compensate for this, including handbooks and manuals for specific models.

In addition to this, and while packed with advice from many professional sources, it remains the final decision of the author as to what has been included. To this end it is not inconceivable that some readers may disagree with some of the contents.

Disclaimer

While every effort has been made to ensure that the contents of this book are accurate, neither the author nor the publisher accepts any liability for any losses or consequential losses incurred by any persons (or vehicles) as a direct or indirect result of reading or acting on the advice contained within this book.

In addition, it is recommended that particular care is exercised when standing near any moving (or stationary) mechanical or structural vehicle parts and that the reader also shows some restraint in the execution of the relevant tests when inspecting another's car. Finally, persons are advised *not* to rely upon the use of a simple jack to support a vehicle while examining underneath. Axle stands, driving ramps or a professional hoist should be used instead.

Acknowledgements

I would like to extend my thanks to all who have helped in the preparation of this edition and, in particular, the following:

Dennis Bradley, Hartwell Ford, London SE13; Phil Mobsby, Ford Technical Division, Walsall; Uncle Len, Mark Transport Co., Green St, Green: Metropolitan Police Service, Orpington CPO; David Rutter; Solotec, Bromley; and not forgetting my favourite Fords: CJN 683T, UKM 741X, ELU 181T, and BEH 317Y particularly, for helping to reveal much along the way.

Some of the material in chapters 6 and 10 has been derived from a book by John Pritchard entitled *The Motorist and the Law – A Guide to Motorists' Rights* (Penguin Books, 1987), now out of print. I am indebted to that book for its clear approach to an otherwise tricky subject.

Introduction

The Purpose of This Book

This book is intended to help you make the right choice when buying a second-hand car or van, and is aimed mainly at the non-mechanically minded. I hope to prove that by following a step-by-step approach, you can confidently choose the most suitable car for your needs and avoid the costly mistake of buying a bad one.

It is not intended as a mechanics' manual, nor will it burden you with overcomplicated and unnecessary technical jargon. The need for such a guide arose in fact from the time I was looking to buy my second car and realized, to my despair, that genuine and inexpensive sources of good advice were quite thin on the ground. The advice I ended up with was of the kind that most used-car seeking people seem to get at one time or another: too technical to understand and remember, or full of half-truths and half-baked theories from enthusiastic would-be mechanics who often disappeared when their help was needed most.

For many of you who already know some of what to look for in a used car – and quite likely have a practised routine – let this book serve both as a useful reminder to what you already know and as a basis from which to broaden your knowledge for next time.

This book will show you:

- The best time to buy second-hand and how to raise the money (chapter 1)
- How to choose the right car for you (chapter 1)

- What you can expect from a used car and why it is important to know its history (chapter 2)
- What a price guide will tell you (chapters 2 and 10)
- How to check the structural and mechanical soundness of a car, and where to look for additional sources of help (chapers 3 and 5)
- How to test-drive a used car (chapter 4)
- Your legal rights when buying second-hand, and what to do when the seller will not help (chapter 6)
- How to cope with dealers and sales talk (chapter 7)
- How to buy (and sell) at auctions (chapter 8)
- Nine things you must do immediately upon buying a used car *if you want to save money*, and how to cut your fuel bills in half (chapter 9)
- How to sell your existing car more quickly and profitably using proven techniques, and the legal obligations that bind you (chapter 10).

Happy hunting
Philip Turner, September 1994

1 When, How and What to Buy

1.1 The Second-hand Car Market

In 1994 the Society of Motor Manufacturers and Traders reported a figure of nearly 28 million vehicles on Britain's roads, of which some 24 million were cars. The majority of cars are second-hand and the market is steadily increasing year by year.

Second-hand car sales are big business; thousands change hands every day of the week, through both private sales and car dealers. The motor trade, and in particular the used-car trade, does not enjoy the best of reputations among the general public but it would be fair to say that this is the fault of a minority of bad dealers. The vast majority are honest and reliable. The difficulty for the customer is knowing who those few that should be avoided are, and eliminating unnecessary risk.

There are several reasons why buying a used car can be a gamble and most relate to attempts by previous owners to save money. Successive owners – less likely than the original buyer to be able to afford full maintenance – may take the attitude that all but essential repairs can wait, or they might extend the service interval, or go to the wrong people for help. All this can have a telling effect on a car's long-term performance and economy.

In fact it is usually very difficult to know a car's true history; in other words, the way in which it has been driven and looked after. And while it is true that in the course of everyday driving a fair percentage of cars will suffer bodywork damage through accident or careless-ness, and that some will be totally written off in serious collisions, there is simply no reason why a car bought brand new cannot last a good fifteen years or more in sound mechanical and driveable condition, irrespective of the number of previous owners. Study carefully the next time you see an early 1970s car in good condition that appears to be driving well – there are a few around, but should such longevity be that remarkable?

1.2 The Best Times to Buy

The motor trade most definitely responds to seasonal fluctuations. The motor show in the autumn, for instance, tempts many people to buy earlier than they usually need and this creates a better-than-average selection of used cars for sale. The same is true of January and August, the times when cars change their year of registration or prefix letter, respectively.

Most second-hand buying is done in the spring and summer when lighter evenings afford better viewing opportunities and people are beginning to think more about excursions and summer holidays. For these reasons prices are generally higher than at other times of the year; salesmen take advantage of the public willing-ness to buy.

Seasonal change also influences the sale of certain types of car. The sale of sporty models and convertibles, for instance, will increase in the spring, while the converse is usually true for off-road or four-wheel-drive cars, which sell better in late autumn.

Winter is therefore the best time to buy if only

because demand is much lower and the trade slack: Christmas preparations, poor weather and a general lack of incentive to drive for pleasure means that fewer cars will be sold and, therefore, prices will be more open to negotiation.

1.3 Raising the Money

There are several recognized means of raising money to buy a car and the merits of each, depending on personal circumstances, are reviewed below:

Savings

This is old-fashioned but probably the best way to buy a large item since you have the money ready; get to own the car immediately; and do not have to pay any interest. At least by using as much of your own money as you can, you'll be reducing the size of any repayments you do have to make – particularly significant if you need a borrowing period of two or more years.

Loans/Overdraft

Unless you know when you'll have the funds in to replenish a loan, you will be paying dearly to borrow. Always agree a sum with your bank or building society first, since the repayments on agreed compared with unauthorized overdrafts can be markedly different. Other loans from banks and building societies can come in the form of a personal loan and are usually subject to your income. Some offer tailored car-loan packages and possibly preferential rates to existing customers. Even if you are not a member of that bank or building society you can still be tempted with generous incentives that might include a free one-year breakdown subscription with a main motoring organization; premium discounts from particular insurance companies; and/or discounts from fast-fit tyre, battery and exhaust outfits. Some packages may be more suitable than others, so it is worth getting plenty of quotes.

Finance groups offer loans at various rates of repayment, some requiring collateral, for example, a house, in the case of a secured loan; however, some do offer unsecured loans but with higher repayment premiums. You can find details of these companies in both the local and national press.

If you are considering a loan remember that there are two different rates of interest and you should understand the difference between them. The flat rate (based on bank base rates), which is the most often quoted, is subject to fluctuation. The other, annual percentage rate or APR, is the rate that you will actually repay. It is a compounded package fixed for the duration of the loan, for example, over twelve, twenty-four or thirty-six months, and is the rate you need to compare.

Dealer Finance

A dealer may offer you a finance package such that you can repay in convenient or 'easy' terms but what you need to ensure is that those 'easy' terms are both convenient and affordable to you! After all, any loan can appear manageable and sufficiently small if prolonged over a fair period of time. Some dealerships even offer 0 per cent financing which even appears to save you money: in reality, such arrangements are likely to increase the deposit required, compromise your discount and dictate a fairly rapid repayment schedule. In recessionary times, though, you may have more room to manoeuvre. *A further, yet little publicized condition of*

*obtaining dealer finance is that you take out fully compre-
hensive insurance, perhaps a lot more expensive than the
third party, fire and theft cover that you had originally
budgeted for. Check you can afford it.*

There is also the possibility of borrowing from a
group such as the AA, which you don't have to be a
member of in order to qualify for their motor-loan
package.

Immediate Family

Consider the possibility of borrowing from family or
friends. You could offer to repay them in instalments as
you would a bank or building society except at a lower
interest. In this way you both benefit: you with the
cheaper (and possibly more flexible) borrowing and
they by getting some return on the money they lent
you.

1.4 Choosing a Car to Suit Your Needs

What kind of car do you really need? This may be
altogether different from the car you would really like
and, for the majority of people at least, the choice will
be something of a compromise. Today there are many
different models of a similar type available and often
little to choose between them.

The following are some of the main factors you may
be considering:

- Purchase price and potential resale value
- Running costs: engine size, maintenance, insurance
  and type of fuel
- Size of car: sub-compact (Fiesta, Nova); compact
  (Escort, Astra); mid-size (Sierra, Cavalier); or full-
  size (Granada, Carlton)

- Body type: saloon, hatchback, estate, convertible, coupé
- Type of use: business, family, general run-around
- Annual mileage: Continental travel, etc.

■ HOT TIP ■

Be wary of choosing a car on the basis of an image you want to project. Choosing an expensive car or one in poor condition can cost you a fortune.

1.5 Engine Size and Comfort

Do you *need* that 3.0-litre gas guzzler to get you down to the shops and back? If you do you will be getting no more than about 15–16 mpg in town traffic even with the benefit of a tuned engine. On the other hand, if you do a lot of long-distance motorway driving, and possibly overseas trips, is it really practical to buy a 1.0-litre Metro or Fiesta? – and there are some with GB nationality stickers! While appearing to make a saving on fuel, these cars would give you a less comfortable ride at speed over long distances than the more robust, deluxe Ford Granada, Volvo or Mercedes top models which, along with the greater weight, have vastly improved suspension, longer wheelbase, better seating and more sophisticated extras. Also, larger engines tend on average to last longer than small ones because they run at lower revs.

An automatic gearbox may be worth serious consideration if your driving is mainly in urban areas. There is a small, yet significant fuel-consumption penalty – however, this can be markedly reduced if the gearbox is used with efficiency and restraint (see 9.9). Automatic gearboxes are more expensive to replace. On the other hand there is no clutch to wear out and be replaced, and automatic gearboxes are now very reliable.

1.6 Running Costs

Many people considering buying a second car tend to look for something quite small, leaving the larger, more powerful family car for heavier duties. The smaller one, which will be doing a lower mileage, is usually ideal for around town, stop-start traffic and easy parking. If this is the kind of thing you have in mind you might consider one of the smaller, mass-produced hatchbacks that are relatively cheap to service and maintain and also require lower insurance premiums.

Cars with good aerodynamic shapes are slightly better on fuel economy than taller, bulky or boxy-shaped cars. Remember that even a roof-rack causes aerodynamic drag, adding around 4 per cent to your fuel bill. Note also that the larger-engined version of a particular model

HOT TIP

While considering how much you should pay for your next used car, remember that the initial outlay is not a very good indication of what the car is likely to cost to run. You should especially beware of picking up a large or deluxe car cheaply only to discover that it consumes vast quantities of fuel, that its insurance rating is prohibitive, or that replacement parts are either hard to come by or very expensive.

may not necessarily use significantly more fuel than the smaller version, especially if you often carry passengers and baggage – the larger engine is working less hard for any given speed. Check the car handbook or the Department of Energy's fuel-consumption figures. Frequent servicing, correct front-wheel alignment and correct tyre pressures of the larger-engined model can offset an mpg advantage of an inadequately maintained smaller engine.

1.7 Insurance Group

In assessing initial costs, consider the likely insurance-group rating that the car will be assigned to. You can find this out from a good price guide but remember that insurance ratings not only vary from company to company but are also subject to more complex factors such as age and experience of driver, personal driving record and even the area of the country where you live and intend to use the car – for example, whether you are in a metropolitan area or deep in the countryside (and recent changes now mean that the full postcode will be taken into account when deciding a high- or low-risk area). Engine size is also important since larger-bodied cars are considered more likely to be involved in a collision. Also, newness, present value, the likelihood of theft, cost of replacement panels, whether or not an alarm or immobilizer is fitted and whether the car is a high-performance model, as well as the type of use to which the car will be put – social, domestic and pleasure or business – will all contribute to the insurance premium you'll pay.

Fuel-injected and turbo-charged engines can vastly increase your premiums. You would do well to obtain quotes from several companies before deciding the best deal. It may even pay you to go direct with the company, since in this way you could cut out much of the insurance-broker fee and make yourself a considerable saving.

There are twenty insurance groups to which a car may be assigned and these chiefly relate to some of the above factors including: size of car and engine, popularity, trim level and, among other things, ease of obtaining spares.

An example from each group is given below, while the figure in brackets refers to the previous insurance-group rating under the old nine-group system.

1.	Citroën 2CV 6 Dolly saloon	(1)
2.	Mini Mayfair 1.0-litre saloon	(1)
3.	Austin/Rover City 1.0-litre hatchback	(1)
4.	Fiat Panda 4x4 3-door hatchback	(2)
5.	Lada Riva 1300 GL saloon	(3)
6.	Vauxhall Astra Belmont 1.4 LX saloon	(3)
7.	Rover 214S hatchback	(4)
8.	Peugeot 309 1.9 GLD hatchback	(4)
9.	Austin Maestro 1.6 HL hatchback	(4)
10.	Ford Sierra Sapphire 2.0 GL saloon	(5)
11.	Ford Granada 2.3 LX estate	(5)
12.	Mercedes-Benz 190D saloon	(6)
13.	Ford Granada 2.9i Ghia hatchback	(7)
14.	Ford Capri 2.8i fastback	(7)
15.	Audi Quattro 2.8E saloon	(−)
16.	Saab 900 turbo saloon (16 valve)	(8)
17.	BMW 325i SE saloon	(8)
18.	Jaguar XJS 3.6 coupé	(9)
19.	Nissan 300 ZX Targa 2 + 2 turbo	(9)
20.	Porsche 911 Carrera Sport Cabriolet	(9)

1.8 Types of Car Design and General Considerations

Essentially, there are five basic categories of car design: saloons; hatchbacks; estates or station-wagons; sports, coupés and convertibles; and multi-purpose vehicles (MPVs), including four-wheel-drive vehicles and people carriers. Your choice will depend on your needs but there may be overlap in some of these categories. For example, a sports hatchback, such as an Astra SRi or Escort XR3i, may well give you good performance, four or five seats and some benefits of an estate (opening tailgate, fold-down rear seats), while others, such as the Vauxhall Calibra 4x4 turbo, will offer a coupé interior, saloon-type boot, split/fold rear seats and some off-road capability, so there can be quite a diversity of choice in model types and you may find that you needn't necessarily compromise much, if at all.

■ HOT TIP ■

With estate cars in particular you need to examine the roof/roof-rack guttering: checking for dents, nicks, scratches and rust there, and also badly scuffed trim in the loading area, could tell you that the car has had previous use as a workhorse.

Check also for leaks at the tailgate hinge, rust at the base, and also that the tailgate can stay up of its own accord. Once you have permission, a simple test worth doing is to throw a bucket of water or hose over the area and watch for leaks.

If you are thinking of buying a convertible, look closely for signs of the hood leaking (either currently or in the past) as this can cause serious floor pan/chassis corrosion. Check also that the hood lowers and raises easily and that all fixings and studs are satisfactory. Replacement hoods are readily available though from specialist hood manufacturers, with prices starting at about £700. Convertibles are more prone to vandalism and possible theft so where you live and park may have a bearing on your purchase decision. Insurance may also prove more expensive than for an equivalent saloon car.

1.9 Fuel-injection Models

These were pioneered in the early 1950s but have only seen widespread introduction in Britain since the 1980s. Here the carburettor is replaced by a system that relies on an exactly metered amount of fuel being mixed with the correct air volume at the right moment. The benefits include greater fuel efficiency, a cleaner burn (and therefore less harmful exhaust emission) and enhanced reliability and performance.

Fuel-injected models must be maintained properly, and if you are thinking of buying one second-hand check for a thorough service history; regular servicing with oil, fuel and air filter changes are important. When driving, be careful not to let the fuel tank drop to zero – dirt and dust sucked into the system can upset its efficiency.

The fuel-injection components (which comprise many non-serviceable parts) can be expensive to replace. A point to watch on older second-hand models (those having done say 60,000–70,000 miles) is that the fuel pumps, sensors and relays linked to the central control unit can be the first to fail and when this happens the system may go out of phase, leading to excessive fuel consumption. Generally with fuel-injection models the picture is fairly black and white; they work either very well or hardly at all.

1.10 Turbo-charged Models

Turbo-charger units are apparatuses fitted mainly to top-of-the-range models in order to improve performance. The unit is fitted to the exhaust system and works by directing air under pressure to the carburettor or fuel-injection unit and, by mixing with more fuel, helps to increase power output. Such engines usually have more robust components, especially the pistons, piston rings and exhaust valves, to withstand the greater pressures and heating inherent in the system.

When buying a turbo model, check the frequency of the service intervals to date – they should be frequent. With serious neglect a turbo unit can disintegrate, causing untold damage to the engine. Replacement units can cost around £500 plus labour. Regular engine oil and filter changes are critical, as is the use of a top-quality motor oil, due to the high operating temperature of a turbo.

1.11 Colour

Colour choice is obviously a personal matter though it is worth noting that bright, light and glossy finishes are safer than colours such as black, dark blue, dark grey, etc., which tend not to stand out quite so clearly against misty and overcast backgrounds.

HOT TIP

When considering the eventual resale of a car, remember that it is the smaller, mass-produced brightly coloured ones that appear to retain most value.

You might find the car of your choice but not like the colour. A respray is an option but a quality respray is expensive – a poor finish will severely reduce the car's value, and there is the likelihood of the paintwork cracking, splitting and peeling within perhaps a matter of only a few months. In any case, will the new colour match the interior trim? Will you respray in the boot and under the bonnet (extra cost)? And will future potential purchasers think the car has been resprayed to conceal accident damage, corrosion or, worse still, a car that's been recently stolen?

1.12 Model Upgrades

Car manufacturers frequently upgrade the specification and styling of their model ranges, so check to see if the model you are interested in was the last of its range –

you may be able to buy a much-improved model for only a little extra money.

In fact by researching the track record of your chosen model you will be able to identify the years in which poor examples were manufactured. For example, the years in which the bodywork was particularly prone to corrosion or paint-fade, or in which the steering or suspension design had resulted in a major safety recall. Bear in mind, too, that it can take a manufacturer several production years to rectify technical defects and so choosing a late model ought to reflect the peak of development in the range.

1.13 Type of Fuel

Diesel or petrol? In recent years diesel has become a more acceptable fuel for private cars with the advantage that it can give up to 25 per cent more efficiency (it releases its energy more quickly than petrol and also gives a cleaner burn). It is cheaper to refine than petrol and retails for a correspondingly lower price, contains no lead additive and is considered to be more friendly to the environment. And although diesel cars are still very much in a minority (approximately 5 per cent, SMMT figure, 1992) they do offer several other import-ant advantages over their petrol-burning counterparts. For example, by using a simpler, unconventional igni-tion system, cold starts need not be dependent on damp weather; the more durable engines can – when properly driven and maintained – achieve record mileages and life expectancy, up to 300,000 miles is not unheard of for a passenger car.

The disadvantages are that second-hand diesel cars are costlier (due to their more complex engines) and noisier than their petrol equivalents; are somewhat sluggish in performance; and the fuel is messy to handle. This has limited their appeal to only a small part of the market. However, diesels are much more popular in Europe, which may be an indication of future trends. (See also 3.3.)

1.14 Leaded or Unleaded?

More and more new cars recently have been manufactured to run on unleaded petrol and since 1989 all have. Some older cars (built since 1976, in fact) are able to run on it either exclusively or mixed with four-star, for example, three fills with unleaded and the fourth with leaded; some can be converted to use unleaded at little or no cost, while some cannot be at all, which can make choosing a particular second-hand model that you would prefer to run on unleaded petrol rather complicated. However, let us look briefly at the two types of petrol and what determines whether or not your potential second-hand choice can be converted to run on unleaded.

Lead is an *additive* which is given to petrol to enhance its performance and to protect engine valves from excessive wear, but which for a long time has been known to cause considerable harm, particularly to children. In 1985 the lead content in petrol was actually reduced without significant loss of performance and in 1986 unleaded petrol, at somewhere between a three- and four-star rating, achieved limited introduction throughout the country. However, while a tremendous break-through, unleaded petrol is still perhaps not as environ-mentally friendly as many of us are conditioned to believe. True, if lead is not actually added to petrol then clearly the air we breathe will be cleaner; but this should really only be considered the first step in reducing widespread exhaust pollution since there are also deadly carcinogens (cancer-producing agents) present in petrol, the hydrocarbon benzene, for example.

A second step involves the recent introduction of the catalytic converter which, by utilizing a ceramic filter in the exhaust system, is able to change the nature of toxic pollutants to less harmful (and even safe) emissions (though it can take a good four or five miles for the cat to reach its operating temperature and, until this has happened, the exhaust emissions will be leaving the tailpipe untreated). Note that if you buy a car equipped with a catalytic converter you *must* use unleaded petrol to avoid damaging the filter.

It is possible to convert most cars from leaded to unleaded petrol. The main change involves an alteration to the ignition timing but on some cars (certain Volvos, for example) the cylinder head may need attention too and, in others, the valves must be changed (because of the poor lubricative properties of unleaded). The huge expense involved in making such adjustments would make such a car neither a cheap nor a viable option.

Before buying a particular second-hand model, make a point of asking at an appropriate main-dealer garage if conversion will be cheap and straightforward, or even if they will do it free of charge for you. You will need to quote the year (age) of the car, engine size and whether it is a fuel-injected model or carburettor-fed. You will also be told whether you need to use a mixture of unleaded and leaded afterwards.

A selling-point of unleaded petrol is that it is cheaper than conventional four-star, but you have to check that the car using unleaded petrol has a similar mpg figure to the car running on four-star and is not actually using more fuel.

2 General on Used Cars

▉▉▉ Introduction

Before we begin a full structural and mechanical survey
on a prospective car, we might learn from what the
statistics tell us about the general condition of used
cars. In doing so we should uncover the reasons for
differences in repair costs for both recent and older
models, understand the importance of determining a
car's history and former uses and learn how to read a
good price guide to maximum effect.

Reliability Report on Used Cars: Common Faults

Included in a popular consumer magazine published in
1988 (*Which?* magazine) was an article that highlighted
the main defects and faults you could expect to find in a
range of new and used makes of car. Problems with
brand-new cars need not concern us here; however, the
used cars were those models over three years old and
those over six, with models over eight years not considered in the survey. Figure 1 represents a summary of
that reliability report and identifies the more common
components that would need either part or total replacement or that would require some attention, if only
cosmetic.

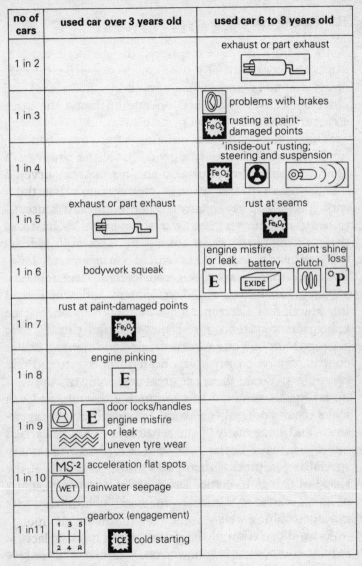

no of cars	used car over 3 years old	used car 6 to 8 years old
1 in 2		exhaust or part exhaust
1 in 3		problems with brakes rusting at paint-damaged points
1 in 4		'inside-out' rusting; steering and suspension
1 in 5	exhaust or part exhaust	rust at seams
1 in 6	bodywork squeak	engine misfire or leak battery clutch paint shine loss
1 in 7	rust at paint-damaged points	
1 in 8	engine pinking	
1 in 9	door locks/handles / engine misfire or leak / uneven tyre wear	
1 in 10	acceleration flat spots / rainwater seepage	
1 in 11	gearbox (engagement) / cold starting	

Figure 1 *Defects and faults commonly found in a cross-section of used cars*

Recent Used Cars

With possibly a few exceptions, the methods used to assess the condition of a used car do not depend much on its age, since both young cars (under five years) and older ones (over ten years) operate on much the same structural and mechanical principles.

What you should be building into your spending limit, though, is not only a good idea of the newer car's likely running costs, but also an idea of what it could cost to repair if and when it malfunctions. For older cars (pre-1985, say) many second-hand and recondi-tioned parts may not be overly expensive to buy and their fitting may quite often be accomplished by the owner. In cars manufactured since around 1986, however, there have been considerable technological advances, including the development and widespread introduction of electronic ignition, fuel injection, engine management systems, electronic warning lights, electric mirrors, windows and sun-roofs, air-conditioning, cruise control, catalytic converters, heated front seats and trip computers. While these are great achievements they are by no means essential to comfortable driving, and can make repairs not only awkward but prohibitively expen-sive – and since many of the repairs may only be carried out by a main dealer who can afford the necessary specialist equipment, then perhaps this is telling of the shape of things to come. Incidentally, the use of many of these extras contributes to your fuel bill, adding mileage-robbing weight.

As an illustration of the dilemma of replacing even a regular component in a newer car, consider a fan heater arrangement: in some older cars this might be a half-hour job due to the reasonable accessibility of the part, which is likely to cost in the region of £65. In more modern cars the same replacement can cost you up to an additional twelve hours' labour, whether it is done by a main dealer *or* smaller outfit, because the dashboard may have to be completely removed in order to do so. If you consider even the conservative labour charge of £35 per hour then you can expect this type of job to set you back some £400–£500! This is not to suggest that repair bills on all younger second-hand cars are always going to be astronomical or that they will be dirt cheap on older cars, only that you would do well to examine realistically the value of the extras, your requirements and your budget beforehand.

2.1 What You are Buying in a Used Car

You can never be 100 per cent certain that the used car you will buy is going to be good value and even with the benefit of a thorough vehicle inspection you will only be *reducing* the risks, however significantly. After all, it has been known for even brand-new cars to have some pretty serious inherent imperfections.

The commodity you are actually buying is the *economical life* left in the car by the previous owner(s). You could define the economical life of a car in terms of the use you can take from it without having to make expensive replacements or repairs outside of normal, regular servicing and maintenance.

When inspecting a car's overall condition and in assessing anything that might need replacing you must bear in mind that the older it is, and the more use it has had, the more attention it will be likely to need. However, just because an older car is going to need two new tyres, a replacement head gasket and a major service does not necessarily make it a bad buy. As a general rule of thumb, you should expect to spend an amount in putting things right that corresponds to the price you paid for it in the first place. For example, with a car priced at £500–£1,000* (probably a 1978–82 model) you might expect to pay around £500 in repairs that could be of a structural, mechanical or electrical nature. A newer car (1983–88) priced between £1,000–£4,000* might need an additional 20–30 per cent of this initial outlay to make it serviceable. Repairs on the most recent second-hand cars, built between 1989–93, for which you might have paid in the region of £4,000–£9,000,* might account for some 10 per cent of this figure. The moral of this is that although the 10 per cent figure quoted for the most recent second-hand cars might be the same as the 50 per cent or more figure in the older ones, the reason you're paying it is because of the longer total life you expect to get out of the latter. And you should make allowance for these kinds of figures in your budget.

It is also most important to decide in your own mind what it is you're prepared to accept in a car *before* you buy it since people's perception of 'used' can differ enormously, particularly when a car is being advertised as in 'excellent' condition. One person may find minor imperfections a serious letdown (for example, driver's seat becoming worn, central locking not working or rust beginning to form on the wheel arches). Another may see this same car as a perfectly satisfactory acquisition.

Depreciation

One school of thought, quite justifiable in its own way, suggests that you never really get true value for money

*These figures refer to approximate second-hand price ranges that you might expect for a cross-section of models.

with a used car when you compare what you take from it with what you have to put back in terms of running costs and repairs. Depreciation is more or less inevitable since many of the items representing this loss, including dealer and manufacturer profits, car tax, delivery, number-plates and VAT charges, are mainly not passed on to successive buyers. And while there are rough-and-ready guidelines to estimate the rates of depreciation for a certain car within a particular class and how much it could be worth after a certain amount of mileage and use, there are two good reasons why you shouldn't pay too much attention to this. Firstly, you are choosing a car now which you have decided will suit your immediate and foreseeable future needs and is the best you can afford. Secondly, it is unlikely that you could begin to predict accurately the resale value any number of years from now – assuming the model to be in fashion still! – and when the time does come for you to sell you can be sure that the final selling price will not be fixed. Generally, cars which depreciate slowly (hold their value) include those in high demand and with 'good image', for example, the Mercedes-Benz 190 or BMW 300-series, or those subject to import quota restrictions: the Toyota MR2, for instance. An example of a high depreciator might include the Renault 21, a fine car mechanically, but its poorly perceived image has meant low demand and dramatically plummeting second-hand values – a shrewd used-car purchase, therefore.

In all of this, there is a *very* general maxim you can use to help in the depreciation battle, which is to buy an approximately three-year-old car (such that the main depreciative losses will have already been paid for by the first owner) and to run and keep it for a further three years, then selling before any major mechanical or other problems appear. In this safe, albeit initially dear ploy you can still sell for a respectable sum, having in the meantime ensured largely predictable running costs.

2.2 Determining a Vehicle's History: Former Keepers and Uses

Let us assume that you have spotted a car you like, perhaps on a dealer's forecourt. What should you do first? Well, before going much further with a structural or mechanical survey (covered in chapter 3), and certainly before you think of test-driving, you should proceed by asking the dealer or private seller some pointed questions in order to determine the car's history and likely former uses.

Preliminary Checks

Preferably you will address the owner, but a dealer – unless he bought from an auction – should have some idea of a car's history from the person who traded it in to him. It is in his interest to do so.

■ HOT TIP ■

Ask to see the vehicle registration document (see figure 5) and glance at the number of previous owners the car has had. If there have been two or three in as many years* then forget the car since for some probably very expensive reason each one could not wait to get rid of it quickly enough.

---

*The vehicle registration document will not directly tell you the recency of all the owner changes, but this is something that can be found out.

If the number is acceptable, make a mental note of the last-recorded owner's or company's address (you can get their phone number from directory inquiries and call them later if need be). That person should have handed over all the relevant records that he had, including MOT certificates, repair bills and service receipts. If it is not a company car and it is not immediately obvious what it has been used for, then ask. For example, a pool car provided for the use of everybody in the division of a company – even if registered in one man's name – may have been subject to some pretty flagrant abuse. Likewise if an old lady has used it for her twice-weekly shopping trips two miles down the road, you can expect a multitude of problems to be brewing; including frequent cold starts rapidly wearing away the cylinder bores and exhaust, high carbon build-up and uneven mechanical wear. In either of these cases you are likely to have landed yourself a bad buy but you will have saved yourself any further disappointment by asking the right questions.

Company Cars

Around 11 per cent of all cars presently on the road are or have been company owned and in 1993 as many as 56 per cent were fleet cars (SMMT figures, 1994).

If the car was company owned, then find out how many drivers it had. If only one, then try to determine this person's age. A young, aggressive rep may have given fairly hard treatment to his car. On the other hand a middle-aged driver, especially if he drove something a bit more upmarket, is likely to have treated the car with more respect – something that necessarily would have come from a good few years of driving experience. This is, of course, only a generalization.

Some company cars can be good buys, especially the younger three- or four-year-olds. Regular long-distance motorway journeys made by a solitary driver means that the car will have been operating at optimal working temperatures, thus minimizing mechanical wear and tear. Servicing would most certainly have been up to the mark and any malfunctions would have been spotted and rectified as they occurred. Remember that young company cars have to be that much more dependable than the average private car, for obvious reasons. In the case of a rep's car check the interior – the upholstery fabric, carpets, interior trim, etc. (see figure 4). Do you notice an overall cleanliness or even newness about it? What about the state of the pedal rubbers – how worn? Peel back the carpet and inspect the floor pan – is the floor the same colour as the carpet or has it been repainted? And how about the back seat – has it ever been used? Was the boot used much either, and is it clean now? Next the doors; they should hang properly and shut with a characteristic clunk. Check them all.

◼ HOT TIP ◼

Check for signs that the car has been used as a taxi or minicab, in particular for signs of hard use: very high mileage, grubby interior, radio or phone attachment points, very worn pedal rubbers and driver's seat, taxi-for-hire plate attachment points including drill holes on either or both the front or rear bumpers. Generally a taxi (hackney carriage) will have led a very hard mechanical life. If in doubt about the vehicle's former uses, contact the previous owner(s).

For some companies it may be policy to sell when the car is three years old since they may not want the complications of spending on any parts that might have failed the car its first or subsequent MOT(s). These cars can prove particularly good buys, since a well-looked-after car only three years old should fly through its MOT. Other firms hang on to a car for longer, say seven or eight years from new, until they feel they have got the full working life out of the car, and then relinquish it the day that it does give problems.

◼ HOT TIP ◼

Do beware of company cars of this age group since, if particularly hard driven, it will be you that picks up the full tab for any of the necessary repairs and replacement parts.

2.3 Mileage

Take a look at the recorded mileage and do not be immediately put off it if seems high since, as we have seen, regular, consistent motorway journeys may have left the car in excellent mechanical condition (along with regular maintenance and good driving habits of course).

Clocked Cars

Next you will need to determine whether the mileage on the odometer is true. When the mileage display is wound back to a lower value, the car is said to be clocked and it is done to fool you into thinking the car has travelled several thousand miles fewer than it really has. Clocking takes two forms. Most commonly, the odometer is wound back a few thousand miles, as suggested above, or it is returned to zero mileage. Look very carefully at the figures and study the vehicle registration document. You will see if the mileage tallies roughly with the age of the car and number of owners, or that it at least looks reasonable. For example, a one-owner-from-new car is three years old and has covered 82,000 miles. This is very high mileage (about 27,000 per year – more than double the national average). You would be relieved to find out that this was a company car belonging to one rep only who was constantly on the road, and in this case the mileage is probably accurate. Remember that the average annual national mileage is in the order of 12,000. Now suppose you are looking at a ten-year-old car having had three previous owners and a recorded mileage of 55,000: you would have every reason to be suspicious (the car might even have covered 155,000 miles) but don't be hasty in your conclusions – there could be a good reason for it. Incidentally, individuals who clock their own cars will not be breaking the law *as long as this is declared when they sell or trade them in; however, clocking by dealers is not only illegal, but also a criminal offence* (see chapter 6). *A staggering 25 per cent of all used cars are estimated to be clocked.* Check that the row of figures in the odometer is properly aligned since once a car has been clocked it is extremely difficult to get all the numbers to reappear in step. For example, consider a car whose odometer reads 70,012 miles:

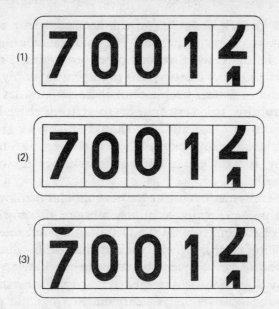

Figure 2 *Milometer (odometer) readings: checking for clocked mileage*

It is only the thousands and tens of thousands mileage columns that you will need to worry about since rewinding by less than 1,000 miles is not going to alter very much from the clocker's point of view.

Both 1 and 2 in figure 2 look reasonable enough, even without perfect alignment, but in 3 the figure 7 especially looks to be quite out of step with the other figures. If this car has been clocked you will not really be sure if it has done 80,000 or even 90,000 miles and you could be gambling on being cheated out of some 20,000+ miles. My advice would be to walk away from a car like this, especially if you discover other signs of deceit.

Another clocking ploy is to paint over part of a figure to make it look like a lower number; for example, to make an 8 look like a 3. You will not necessarily notice this upon casual inspection but imagine your anger when, in the case of an odometer registering 39,500, another 500 miles increases the mileage to 90,000!

If in any doubt, telephone the previous owner who will probably talk very freely, especially if there is no comeback on it for him. He should at least be able to recall the car's approximate mileage when he sold it, but if he is cagey you might wonder whether he clocked it himself.

Sometimes an odometer looks as though it has probably been zeroed; for example, a car of three or four years that displays only 2,500 miles. Firstly, look for evidence of tampering with the unit's housing – it would have had to be removed to get to the clock part – and for any scratched or damaged screw heads that might betray a recently removed instrument from the dashboard. However, if changing the odometer has been done for good reason there should be a legitimate receipt to back up anything the seller tells you.

2.4 Documentation

Examine the MOT certificates. The more complete the vehicle's history the better recourse you will have to its true mileage. A five-year-old car will have two MOT certificates and on each one the then current mileage will have been recorded; so check on each one that the interim mileages look feasible for the kind of driving the car will have done. Check the obvious, too – that the present recorded mileage is actually the same or greater than that noted on the latest MOT paper. Figure 3 shows a typical MOT certificate and highlights the important points to examine.

1. Vehicle registration number: check it agrees with *both* front and rear plates on the car.

2. Vehicle identification number (VIN): check agreement with the VIN plate on the car's front slam panel (see figure 17).

3. Certificate validity: look at the date of expiry on the certificate. If less than ten months' MOT remaining, ask to have the car retested at your own expense.

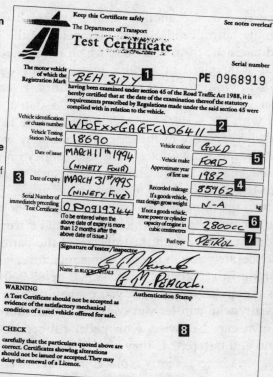

4. Mileage: a useful clue to genuine mileage, this. Ensure that the mileage entered here is *not* greater than that recorded on the odometer – if so, the car could be clocked.

5. General vehicle particulars: make sure all vehicle descriptions in fact relate to the car, for example, make, colour, year of manufacture, engine capacity (**6**) and type of fuel used (**7**).

8. Vehicle testing station (VTS) details: is the testing station authentication stamp (station impress) both present and legible? (If not, the certificate is worthless.) Check that the VTS number corresponds with that on the authentication stamp. Also, is the MOT testing station local to the seller's home – if not, why not? And are the tester's name and signature (**9**) both present and in agreement?

Finally, does the certificate show any alterations – if so, why?

Figure 3 *A typical MOT certificate: important points to examine*

Service Records

Service records are another means by which you can determine faithful mileage. In younger cars the service record takes the form of a book which is stamped when the car is serviced at regular intervals, for example, every six months or 6,000 or 12,000 miles. Even when the car is older, some owners keep a dated receipt issued with the service on which the mileage has been recorded (especially in the case of a company who will have spent possibly a lot of time and money on a rep's or manager's car). You should always ask to see any records that you think are relevant.

Back to the interior for a moment. Take a look at the steering-wheel pattern, which should have worn at a rate commensurate with the mileage. If the pattern was of a deliberately rough texture at manufacture, is it now smoothing in accordance with 48,000 or 88,000 miles? If it is a popular model then you probably know someone locally who will let you compare its condition with their own car. Likewise, with pedal rubbers; do they look old and tattered? If they look brand new then have the old ones been recently replaced in order to convey a false impression of the mileage the car has actually covered?

And what about the presence of seat covers? A seat cover could tell you either that the car has covered a huge mileage and hence the seats are becoming visibly worn and frayed, and/or that the upholstery has been torn, cut or stained, etc. Neither condition being particularly desirable.

There is a school of thought that questions whether you need be concerned at all about clocking in the case of a ten-year-old car since, in nearly all cases, the

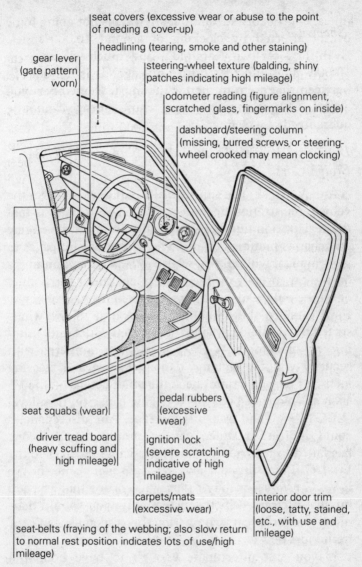

seat covers (excessive wear or abuse to the point of needing a cover-up)

headlining (tearing, smoke and other staining)

gear lever (gate pattern worn)

steering-wheel texture (balding, shiny patches indicating high mileage)

odometer reading (figure alignment, scratched glass, fingermarks on inside)

dashboard/steering column (missing, burred screws or steering-wheel crooked may mean clocking)

seat squabs (wear)

pedal rubbers (excessive wear)

driver tread board (heavy scuffing and high mileage)

ignition lock (severe scratching indicative of high mileage)

carpets/mats (excessive wear)

interior door trim (loose, tatty, stained, etc., with use and mileage)

seat-belts (fraying of the webbing; also slow return to normal rest position indicates lots of use/high mileage)

Figure 4 *Car interior wear to check against the milometer (odometer) reading*

mileage, probably substantial anyway, is not going to be overly affected by clocking of around 10,000 miles. Even for a car two years old – how much will an extra 10,000 miles affect its future mileage? It is the ones in between that seem to matter the most. Remember, you have no obligation to buy a car whose mileage cannot be guaranteed (see chapter 7).

Important Vehicle Identification Numbers (VINs): Stolen Cars

A quick check you must make while you have the vehicle registration document (V5) in your hand is that the registration number-plates tally and that the engine and chassis numbers tie up. The first couple of pages in your manual will tell you where to locate these numbers on the car, usually on the front panel under the bonnet or on the bulkhead (see figure 17) or, in the case of newer Ford cars, on the dashboard at the base of the windscreen. Be particularly vigilant for altered, defaced, missing or unstamped VIN plates, also tampered-with security window etching, damaged door and steering locks. At the same time check the other details on the V5 such as colour of bodywork, engine capacity, trim level (L, GL, etc.) and transmission type. Any discrepancies could indicate a stolen car or simply that someone has failed to report any vehicle particular changes to the DVLC. Point this out and get the seller to notify the DVLC *before* you buy. This will ensure that you are buying a 'clean' vehicle. Incidentally, you should definitely forget a car whose 'log book details can't be found just now'.

If you are unfortunate enough to have bought a stolen car, remember that there is very limited recourse even in innocence. The police, if they trace the vehicle,

1. Owner (or keeper) ID: should agree with who the seller says he is, and also correspond with the address where the vehicle is now.

2. Vehicle registration mark: should tally with *both* front and rear number-plates and MOT certificate, if applicable.

3. Taxation class: if the car was formerly a taxi or minicab, this entry would say 'Hackney carriage' instead of 'private/light goods'.

4. Make, model, specification (trim level) and basic body type of car; also colour and type of fuel required.

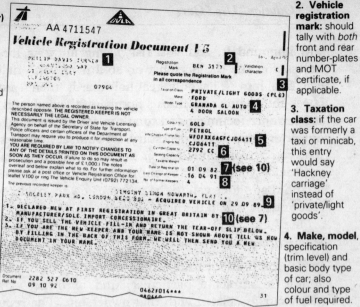

5. Vehicle identification numbers (VINs): should agree exactly with the sequence of letters and numbers embossed on the metal plate located, usually, on the front slam panel (see figure 17). Beware any defacing, burring or alteration of these figures either on the certificate or VIN plate itself. It often implies an 'unclean' car.

6. Engine size: this should correspond with both the badging on the boot or tailgate and, if applicable, the MOT certificate (s).

7. First date of registration: should tally with the registration suffix or prefix letter on the number-plate (for example, 1982 corresponds to an X or Y suffix). See also **10**.

8. Last change of ownership: tells how long the current owner has had the car. If not long, ask why. Also how many former owners? – many in a short time can blow the whistle on a 'bad' car.

9. Previous owner's address: contact the previous owner and ask pointed questions about the car – can help confirm car's true mileage and even whether it has been stolen or accident damaged.

10. Tells if car was *not* new at first registration in the UK. Could be an imported model, rebuilt or even a kit car. See also **7**.

Finally, beware any 'unauthorized alterations' to the document, for example, typewritten additions to the dates, registration number or specification; and in holding the document to the light, a repeating DVLA watermark should ensure that the certificate is authentic.

Figure 5 *The vehicle registration document (or V5): important points to examine*

will impound it, and you risk losing all your money unless you sue the person who sold it to you – if you can find him. The only real safeguards then* are to check the engine and chassis numbers, the name on the registration document and to ask to see the original bill of sale or other ID as necessary. Of course, making sure that you actually purchase *at* the seller's address ought to provide you with sufficient recourse should you need it, and that phone call to the previous owner could even save you the trip in the first instance.

Boy Racers and Madmen

It may be prudent to note that certain types of car do appear to attract a particular kind of owner – and behaviour associated with that ownership. The reputations of several of the smaller, high-performance turbo-charged and fuel-injected hot hatches will attest to this. As a general rule you would probably do best to avoid some of the more gaudy, sporty-looking examples, the type frequently adorned with after-market skirting, spoiler and air dam add-ons, bright 'go faster' stripes or coachlines and bodywork logos (such as roofless, turbo, injection etc.), heavily tinted windscreens, the remnants of powerful stereo systems and, of course, customized with banks of spotlights or lowered suspensions. Indeed, those cars with specially *modified* engines, having perhaps enjoyed many former owners, are among the type of car that will almost certainly have been pushed well beyond

---

* HPI Autodata (0722) 422422, is a service now available to the public nationwide that will be able to tell the buyer of any police interest in the vehicle, whether it has been rebuilt following serious accident damage, or indeed has any finance owing on it. The service costs £15.

their limits. Insurance premiums on them are also likely to be prohibitive.

Suffice it to say the purchase of any used car involves a risk, and *who* you buy from can be as important in the transaction as the example of car itself. Be satisfied that the current owner is someone who you think would have treated the car as you would yourself.

Vehicle Registration

When checking the number-plate details and that the single-letter suffix or prefix corresponds with the age of the car (a list of registration suffix and prefix letters for 1963–2003/4 is given in figure 6), look at the other three-letter sequence in the registration number. It will tell you where the vehicle was first registered; the second two letters (the first is a serial letter) will indicate the town, city or district of registration of the car. Occasionally you can tell a little of the car's history from this; if you buy a car with a three-letter registration series PYY, for instance, the YY indicates registration in Central London. If the registration document records the addresses of the one, two or three previous owners as being in Central London also, then you might infer that the car has been used there for the major part of its life. Such a car would have been driven in mainly stop-start traffic and you could reason fairly that a car driven in a more open, rural area is going to be much more healthy. A minor point, perhaps, but this is all part of the procedure of thoroughly investigating a vehicle's former uses and history, which, as you must now begin to appreciate, will require a little bit of organized effort on your part if you are to minimize your risk of buying anything that is less than good value for money. A list

of two-letter London registration codes is reproduced
in figure 7.

Registration Number-plates

Since 1963 a five- to seven-digit sequence has been
used on car registration plates. Cars registered between
1 January and 31 December would have carried a suffix
letter A, for example, TGF 609A, and for cars in 1964
the suffix letter in newly registered vehicles would have
been B, for example, UMX 218B. In 1967 the new
registration date was changed to 1 August, such that an

Figure 6 *Registration suffix and prefix letters for cars 1963–2003/4*

(Suffixes, to July 1983)		*(Prefixes, from August 1983)*	
A	1.1.63–31.12.63	A	1.8.83–31.7.84
B	1.1.64–31.12.64	B	1.8.84–31.7.85
C	1.1.65–31.12.65	C	1.8.85–31.7.86
D	1.1.66–31.12.66	D	1.8.86–31.7.87
E	1.1.67–31.7.67	E	1.8.87–31.7.88
F	1.8.67–31.7.68	F	1.8.88–31.7.89
G	1.8.68–31.7.69	G	1.8.89–31.7.90
H	1.8.69–31.7.70	H	1.8.90–31.7.91
J	1.8.70–31.7.71	J	1.8.91–31.7.92
K	1.8.71–31.7.72	K	1.8.92–31.7.93
L	1.8.72–31.7.73	L	1.8.93–31.7.94
M	1.8.73–31.7.74	M	1.8.94–31.7.95
N	1.8.74–31.7.75	N	1.8.95–31.7.96
P	1.8.75–31.7.76	P	1.8.96–31.7.97
R	1.8.76–31.7.77	R	1.8.97–31.7.98
S	1.8.77–31.7.78	S	1.8.98–31.7.99
T	1.8.78–31.7.79	T	1.8.99–31.7.2000
V	1.8.79–31.7.80	V	1.8.2000–31.7.2001
W	1.8.80–31.7.81	W	1.8.2001–31.7.2002
X	1.8.81–31.7.82	X	1.8.2002–31.7.2003
Y	1.8.82–31.7.83	Y	1.8.2003–31.7.2004

Central London
HM (for example, KHM 311T), HV, HX, HX, JD, UC, UL, UU, UV,
UW, YE, YF, YH, YK, YL, YM, YN, YO, YP, YR, YT, YU, YV,
YW, YX, YY

South London
GC (for example, AGC 987W), GF, GH, GJ, GK, GN, GO, GP, GT,
GU, GW, GX, GY, MV, MX, MY

North London
BY (for example, D48 XBY), LA, LB, LC, LD, LE, LF, LH, LK, LL,
LM, LN, LO, LP, LR, LT, LU, LW, LX, LY, RK, OY, MC, MD,
ME, MF, MG, MH, MK, ML, MM, MP, MT, MU

Figure 7 *A list of two-letter registration sequences for London-registered cars*

F-registered car would have been so between 1 August 1967 and 31 July 1968. Excluding the letters I, O, Q, U and Z,* letters were used progressively through the alphabet until Y and then the age of a car was denoted by a prefix letter starting with A on 1 August 1983, for example, A418 TUW.

2.5 Summary

Determining a car's history is quite a tricky task. The signs are there but if you are to learn anything of value you must remember to use every available piece of information before concluding anything. *Never conclude anything about a used car from isolated observations.*

*Letters I and Z are used for registering cars in both Northern Ireland and the Republic of Ireland, for example, WWZ would indicate a registration in Belfast while FZI would show a car registered in Dublin. The letter Q implies a kit car or one whose original registration details are missing, or unconventional, for example, an imported or rebuilt car.

In general, when considering a car's history, you should do the following:

- Ask to see both the vehicle registration document and (current and past) MOT certificates, and check the frequency and recency of former owners; make a note of the last owner's name and address
- Ask about the car's previous uses if not already apparent
- Check that the engine and chassis numbers tally with what is recorded on the registration document and also other details, including bodywork colour, engine capacity, number-plates and date of registration
- Check current mileage against previous MOT certificates and refuse a car whose registration details 'cannot be found'
- Check if the car has been clocked by noting any obvious misalignment of the figures in the mileage reading (see figure 2), extremely low mileages (zeroing), painted-over numbers, tampered-with speedometer unit and/or erratic or dysfunctional speedo needle
- Check the interior for signs of wear commensurate with mileage including pedal rubbers, steering-wheel pattern, gear/lever handle, upholstery, headlining fabric, interior velour and trim, front and back seats, boot area and doors. Also, driver's treadboard for scuffing, ignition lock and keys for severe scratching and the seat-belt inertia-reel mechanism for slackness and slow return
- Ask to see any service and repair or maintenance bills – they can help confirm the true mileage
- Approximately one in nine cars is or has been

company owned. When considering one of these, try to determine the number and ages of the drivers, the type of firm that owned it and why they are selling it *now*

● Do not be put off by a high-mileage car – provided regular service, maintenance and repair history is in order you could get a good buy – as you will pay less than you would for a car recording only average mileage

● Try to find out if the car has been garaged at the end of each day's driving – this would have left it in much better overall condition with minimal corrosion

● Investigate the district, town or city of registration and address(es) of the previous owner(s) – find out what you can about the car's life to date.

2.6 What a Used-car Price Guide Will Tell You

Used-car price guides can be a very useful starting-point when investigating the going price of a second-hand car, whether you are buying privately, from a dealer or from auction. They are also the best place to start when you are thinking of selling your own car and are in any case far more reliable than most friends' ill-informed guesswork.

In addition to the used-car price sections found in some motoring magazines, there are two main guides to choose from: *Parker's Price Guide* and *The Motorists' Guide*, (while other, recently launched price guides include *The Motor Trade Guide to Used-car Prices* and *Greenlight's Used-car Prices*) each retailing for around £2 monthly.

Both guides list prices for brand-new cars, too, as

well as featuring market reports, auction site direc-
tories and new- and used-model information.

Categorization

Both guides list cars according to make and at the
beginning of each model is a brief history that details
the months and years of significant improvement to the
model (see figure 8).

Figure 8 *A comparison of the information obtainable from two
of the major used-car price guides: the (Toyota) Lexus LS 400*

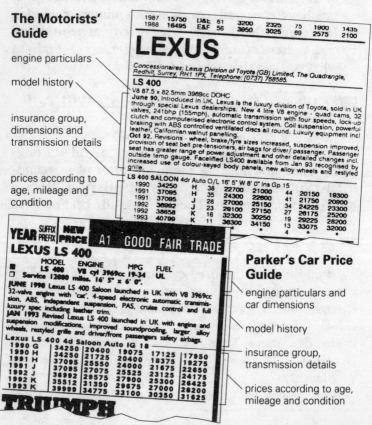

The guides typically cover a ten-year period and, when listing prices, both rate according to: new, A1 (or first class), good, fair (or average) and trade prices; and there is a good description of how you should use these definitions to assess a car's condition. Of the two, possibly *Parker's* bolder columns make identifying the necessary figures that much easier, yet *The Motorists' Guide* provides greater flexibility, with mileages based on differing yearly averages (see figure 8). Both indicate a car's insurance-group rating – very helpful when thinking of switching to a different make or model.

On the whole, both are compact mines of useful information and are a must for anyone wanting to begin the buying process on the right footing.

3 What to Look for Structurally and Mechanically

Introduction

It is not possible to examine every single working (or non-working) part of a car – there are too many of them and there is never enough time. Often it is the case that your anticipated driving life with the car makes a little surface rust, accident damage or some worn elements of the engine insignificant in relation to the price you will be paying.

As a rule you do get what you pay for and although any final decision as to what is or is not acceptable will vary from one individual to the next with any second-hand car you must expect to pay something towards the replacement of parts. However, you will not want to buy a car that needs too much attention initially, nor one that is going to demand regular bonnet-up treatment, with frequent and high garage repair bills.

The following, while similar to what you might expect to be covered in the course of a vehicle inspection, have been selected as relatively simple tests you can do yourself to make a judgement on a used car.

NOTE: Certain components may vary in both appearance and location in different makes and models of car and so it is advisable to buy or borrow a handbook *specific* to the model you are interested in, in order to make their identification easier when conducting the following tests.

A good guide to get is one of the Haynes series, which retails for around £12 from any good motor factor. Do not rule out, however, the likelihood of picking up the very copy you need from a car-boot sale for as little as 35p – I picked up the manual for my present car for only 50p!

■■■ HOT TIP ■■■

Firstly, only ever go to examine a car in good daylight. Showroom light, dusk or the presence of droplets of rainwater all help mask bodywork imperfections such as filler and faded paintwork, thereby making the car appear to be in better external condition than it actually is.

3.1 Structural Pointers

General Impression

In trying to decide how a car has been previously treated, you can gather a surprising amount of detail from an inspection of the bodywork alone. You should take a walk around the car, observing its overall condition and any obvious dents and rusting. Remember that you are not buying a new car and that it is possible at least one of the panels has been either resprayed, repaired or even replaced. If a good job has been done this matters little, but a bad job not only looks tacky but will lose you money when you come to resell.

■■■ HOT TIP ■■■

Beware of a car that looks too clean or low-priced for its age – it could be hiding serious faults.

Rust

Cars registered and driven exclusively in the north of Britain have a reputation for being somewhat rustier than those in the south due to colder winters and subsequent excesses of salt on the road, which assists the corrosion process. Also, certain makes of car have been known to rust prematurely and purchasing one could be asking for trouble (see 1.12).

■■■ HOT TIP ■■■

Serious rusting at structural points may not only mean an MOT failure but could also make the repair of the car so costly that you may even have to scrap it.

Make sure you examine the following points when checking for rust:

- under front and rear bumpers
- valance area
- door panels and sills
- wheel arches
- front and rear wings
- boot lid or tailgate
- fuel tank
- chassis, cross-members and subframes
- floor pan
- roof
- door seams
- suspension mountings
- jacking points
- roof and bonnet edges
- and any exposed interface between two welded points (see figures 9 and 10).

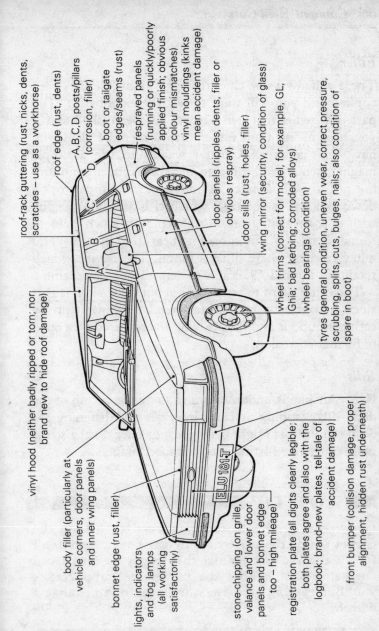

roof-rack guttering (rust, nicks, dents, scratches – use as a workhorse)

roof edge (rust, dents)

A,B,C,D posts/pillars (corrosion, filler)

boot or tailgate edges/seams (rust)

resprayed panels (running or quickly/poorly applied finish; obvious colour mismatches

vinyl mouldings (kinks mean accident damage)

door panels (ripples, dents, filler or obvious respray)

door sills (rust, holes, filler)

wing mirror (security, condition of glass)

wheel trims (correct for model, for example, GL, Ghia; bad kerbing; corroded alloys)

wheel bearings (condition)

tyres (general condition, uneven wear, correct pressure, scrubbing, splits, cuts, bulges, nails; also condition of spare in boot)

vinyl hood (neither badly ripped or torn; nor brand new to hide roof damage)

body filler (particularly at vehicle corners, door panels and inner wing panels)

bonnet edge (rust, filler)

lights, indicators and fog lamps (all working satisfactorily)

stone-chipping (on grille, valance and lower door panels and bonnet edge too – high mileage)

registration plate (all digits clearly legible; both plates agree and also with the logbook; brand-new plates, tell-tale of accident damage)

front bumper (collision damage, proper alignment, hidden rust underneath)

Figure 9 Some important initial considerations when determining a car's overall condition

Filler

There will always be clues to suggest that filler has been applied and you will want to test the extent of it. Tap part of a panel that you suspect has been filled and if you hear a dull thud rather than a metallic clang you have your answer. A better way is to use a simple magnet, which will cling to metal (except aluminium) but not to a filled patch of bodywork. Halfords stock a device known as Spotrot, which is basically a magnet with a scale that gives a high reading when held to sound metal, a medium reading near to hidden rust and a low reading where filler is found. The device, which retails for around £9, is able to detect layers of repaint.

The other point to remember about filler work is that since it contracts, bad winters tend to show it up by eating around it and thus leaving the repaired area open to further corrosion.

Sills

Run your hands underneath and along the length of the door sills, tapping at close intervals and listening for dead sounds that might betray rust or filler. Feel also for holes caused by rusting at an advanced stage.

■ HOT TIP ■

Check the inner sill, too; you need to lift up the carpet inside the car by the driver's seat. And don't forget the jacking points; they must be free from corrosion and enable the car to be supported – you'll be relying on them when needing to change a wheel.

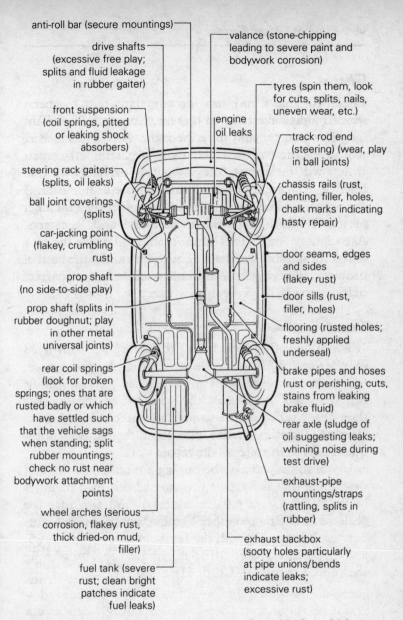

anti-roll bar (secure mountings)

valance (stone-chipping leading to severe paint and bodywork corrosion)

drive shafts (excessive free play; splits and fluid leakage in rubber gaiter)

tyres (spin them, look for cuts, splits, nails, uneven wear, etc.)

front suspension (coil springs, pitted or leaking shock absorbers)

engine oil leaks

track rod end (steering) (wear, play in ball joints)

steering rack gaiters (splits, oil leaks)

chassis rails (rust, denting, filler, holes, chalk marks indicating hasty repair)

ball joint coverings (splits)

car-jacking point (flakey, crumbling rust)

door seams, edges and sides (flakey rust)

prop shaft (no side-to-side play)

door sills (rust, filler, holes)

prop shaft (splits in rubber doughnut; play in other metal universal joints)

flooring (rusted holes; freshly applied underseal)

rear coil springs (look for broken springs; ones that are rusted badly or which have settled such that the vehicle sags when standing; split rubber mountings; check no rust near bodywork attachment points)

brake pipes and hoses (rust or perishing, cuts, stains from leaking brake fluid)

rear axle (sludge of oil suggesting leaks; whining noise during test drive)

exhaust-pipe mountings/straps (rattling, splits in rubber)

wheel arches (serious corrosion, flakey rust, thick dried-on mud, filler)

exhaust backbox (sooty holes particularly at pipe unions/bends indicate leaks; excessive rust)

fuel tank (severe rust; clean bright patches indicate fuel leaks)

Figure 10 *Some important areas to examine with the vehicle on a hoist*

Chassis

Check for dents and also for any signs that a serious
shunt might have reached this far. Chassis rails run the
length of the car and must be right. Any damage here
will upset the car's balance, making it steer off-centre,
which will be obvious during a test drive. Beware of
filler or even weld or chalk marks in the visible part. A
well-repaired chassis – done, for example, by a member
of the VBRA, the Vehicle Builders' and Repairers'
Association (see 6.9 for address) – may still make the car a
perfectly suitable purchase. This is not really the kind of
problem, though, that you would want to have to correct
before you can drive your 'new' car.

Illegal Rebuilds?

It is not actually illegal for a car, having been involved
in a serious collision, to be repaired and offered again
for resale. However, until now there has been no specific
test designed to measure the standard of repair other
than the MOT, which would fail the car if either its
steering, lights or brakes were left affected as a consequence of, or in spite of, the repair work.

If you think you may be buying a rebuilt vehicle, first
determine that the repair was carried out by a member
of the VBRA (see 6.9 for address), and also that the
registration mark and other Vehicle Identification Numbers of the car tally with the registration certificate (V5)
and any other records that might be kept concerning
the vehicle at the DVLC or HPI (see 2.4).

Floorings

■■■HOT TIP ■■■■■■■■■■■■■■■■

Check underneath the front half of the car for floor corrosion and general damage. Feel for dirt and holes as well and for anything that feels like freshly or unevenly applied underbody sealant.

Also check the rear half of the floor and the boot floor, in particular for rippling that may have been caused by an accident.

■■■HOT TIP ■■■■■■■■■■■■■■■■

Damp carpets suggest a possible windscreen, sunroof or door seal leak.

Inspect the condition of the door and windscreen seals; cracked, split or poorly fitting rubber will aid the ingress of water.

Wheel Arches

■■■HOT TIP ■■■■■■■■■■■■■■■■

Again, feel for holes and rust in every crevice, especially at places where mud will have lodged (water and salt in the mud will quickly eat away at metal). Gently peel away at any loose layers and be reassured if you find good metal early on. If layer after layer of rust simply crumbles away then much of the area is rotten and probably beyond repair.

Doors

Look for obvious rusting or filler repairs that could indicate crash damage. If not done properly, filled work shows up as light uneven scratch lines. Look for obvious colour mismatches between adjacent panels, and also for patchy respraying or stripes on door panels that do not line up exactly (see figure 11). Make sure you do this in the right light – a dealer may try to conceal a mismatched panel by parking the car in the shade. Doors should hang properly so check the hinges on each door in turn. Badly closing doors may point to a collision at some time, or it may just be a question of needing adjustment. *Study the lower door panels for signs of paint blistering or bubbling – this will be rust starting from the inside and working its way out. With the doors open, look and feel along the edges and undersides for rust, holes or any gaps between the inside and outside surfaces of the panel.* Finally, check each of the door locks and, if they are controlled by a central-locking mechanism, that all doors respond satisfactorily to it.

Other Panels

Look for filler and resprayed wing surfaces in particular – the corners of any car are the most vulnerable to damage.

Turn next to the tailgate or boot area and note any colour differences (often a respray implies a replacement panel here). Examine the tailgate and carefully scan for paint that might have run during respray and also for local areas that are either flecked with the new colour or else missed, perhaps betraying the car's original finish. As with bodywork that has been refilled, there is always evidence of respraying if you look hard enough. Stand

windows (security window etching present, not defaced)

windows (smooth up-and-down winding operation)

windows (all glass either tinted or else plain – mixture suggests vandalism or theft; stickers may reveal the kind of use or owner; may also be hiding cracks. See also keyholes, damaged locks, multiple keys)

ariel operation (double-check if electric)

sun-roof (tilt/slide operation)

windscreen (tramlines left by windscreen wiper blades)

windscreen (cracks and chips – an MOT checking point)

lights (rusting of reflective backing – an MOT checking point)

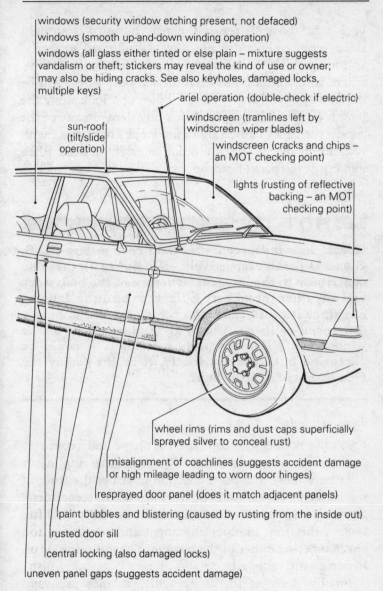

wheel rims (rims and dust caps superficially sprayed silver to conceal rust)

misalignment of coachlines (suggests accident damage or high mileage leading to worn door hinges)

resprayed door panel (does it match adjacent panels)

paint bubbles and blistering (caused by rusting from the inside out)

rusted door sill

central locking (also damaged locks)

uneven panel gaps (suggests accident damage)

Figure 11 *Further detailed visual checks*

back and check to see if the rear bumper is straight since replacements are not always realigned properly, and just behind the bumper check for gaps at any seams where spot-welding has been carried out. These will be the first to rust. Lastly, crouch down and look along the length of the car's bodywork for tiny dents in any of the panels (possibly caused by flying stones or contact with roadside hedges!) which are not so easily noticed when looking at the panel head-on.

Pillars

▰ HOT TIP ▰

Check the windscreen, door and rear pillars (A, B, C and D posts, respectively – see figure 9); these do contribute to the integral structure of the bodywork and any filler found here is likely to be quite dangerous since it could cause the vehicle to fold in even a low-speed collision. Check at the lower half of the windscreen pillar for peeling lacquer. It could be corrosion but, more seriously, it might betray the true extent of a hard shunt.

Inner Panels

Open the bonnet and compare the shape and symmetry of the inner wings (see figure 17). Any rust, rippling or filler here must indicate a collision to either the front of the car or its wings (and you ought to take a second look at the visible part of the chassis bars for damage). Also, look at the front bumper alignment and condition, and check whether either of the headlight or indicator lenses look recently renewed.

Finally, look at the front grille, valance area and lower parts of the door panels for stone-chip marks.

This will tell you if the car has been driven on the motorway a great deal. Bad stone-chipping can leave the bodywork vulnerable to rusting. Many dabs with a paint touch-up stick, though, suggests a caring owner.

Engine Mountings

While the bonnet is open, lean inwards and take a look down the sides of the engine for its mountings, which may appear like small rubber doughnuts. They secure the engine to the bodywork and help minimize vibration. They should not be peeling or split and should, on average last some twelve to fifteen years. A loose or broken mounting will produce noticeable vibrations throughout the cabin interior upon tick-over and excessive lurching when accelerating away from rest. Their retightening is a relatively straightforward task for a garage.

3.2 Mechanical Pointers

Here the picture is less clear cut and your decision to buy is more likely to be swayed by overall condition than by any one single feature of the car in question. For the purpose of this section, mechanical parts are considered to be anything that will wear out and need replacing during the normal course of a car's driving life.

Engine

Get someone else to start the engine for you while you stand at the back with an eye on the exhaust emissions (at the same time, notice how quickly and easily the engine turns over). Blue exhaust smoke points to wear of the piston rings and valve guides. Black clouds mean either too rich a petrol mixture, or that petrol and oil are being burned (see p. 94 for black exhaust smoke and diesels). After running the engine for a few minutes, lift up the bonnet and look for oil escaping – in vapour form – from the filler cap region, dipstick or breather valves. A glance at the mileage will tell you if this is an old engine (perhaps 95,000 miles or more) or one that has been prematurely abused.

Replacement Engines

You may decide that it is only the engine that needs replacing. With an older second-hand car it is unlikely that you are going to want to pay main-dealer prices (£1,000–£2,000) for a reconditioned engine, unless this car is definitely going to mean a lot to you. There are several other outlets offering reconditioned engines; however, the first thing you should decide is whether or not you are actually getting one that's reconditioned *or* rebuilt. Price is quite a good guide in this and, according to some dealers of reclaimed engines, there can be considerable difference. Generally, a rebuilt engine will not carry a guarantee since it is only the parts that needed it that are actually replaced. In reconditioned engines, however, you can be fairly sure that all parts have been appraised, including: the crankshaft, connecting rods, gaskets, pistons, piston rings, timing belts, valve guides and also the reboring of cylinders and proper machining of any parts that need it. As a result you should get a 12,000-mile or one-year guarantee against any major faults. And, finally, if you are considering getting a new engine put in, you would be better off using a member of the FER, the Federation of Engine Remanufacturers, who set the standards for engine remanufacture (see 6.9 for address).

General Running

With the engine on tick-over, listen to its general tone – and, of course, the more experience you have had of hearing the difference between good and bad engines the easier this will be. Listen out for heavy knocking or rattling upon start-up (compared to an initial light tapping that soon disappears) – it signals worn big end bearings and will be expensive to remedy. And while a simple misfire can be easily cured, try to avoid cars whose engines sound lumpy, uneven at idle or laboured when revved.

Oil leaks

Engine oil leaks are usually self-evident, yet finding their source is not always straightforward since whole areas of the engine can be awash. Leaks will manifest themselves at the weakest points. For more specific advice see chapter 9.

Oil Filter

Locate the oil filter (see figure 17). A canister or cartridge approximately four inches in length, it is screwed on to the engine block, in which its function is to trap – and thus prevent the circulation of – impurities carried by the oil. As a rule it should be replaced every 6,000 miles (or six months). Ask when it was last changed. Most privately sold cars will be needing a service but be warned if you see thick, dried-on oil stains smothering the filter casing: the owner might well sing the car's praises but in reality this means a leaking or neglected engine.

Carburettor

If you know that the engine has been recently tuned, you can expect that the carburettor(s) will have seen some adjustment, which should have curbed any erratic idling and stalling shortly after start-up. With the engine ticking over, depress the accelerator pedal (or throttle linkage) in a series of short stabs to test its response: there should be rapid revving, with any hesitancy indicating an acceleration flat spot.

Ignition

Examine the high-tension (HT or ignition) leads that connect from the distributor to each spark-plug and look for any that are loose, frayed or very dirty. Make sure that the spark-plugs are not coated in oil, then unclip and remove the distributor cap and determine that the pick-up points inside are clean and that the rotor-arm arrangement (refer to manual or handbook and see figure 12) is not badly blackened or burned out. These items should all be in A1 condition if the car has had a recent service.

Ignition Warning Light

This should come on and go out immediately the engine fires. If it stays on (or comes on later) it can point to a low battery or alternator, or perhaps suspect circuitry.

Head Gasket

The cylinder head gasket forms a tight seal between the engine block and cylinder head, keeping the oil and water apart.

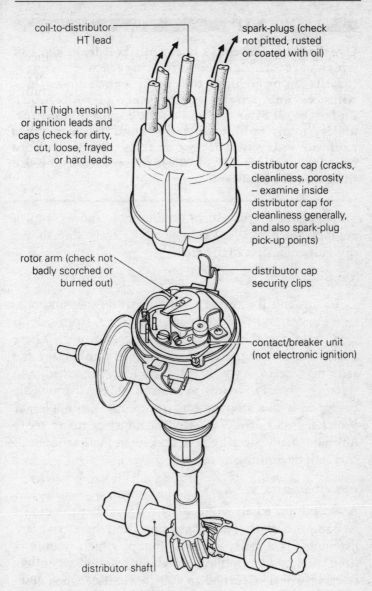

coil-to-distributor HT lead

spark-plugs (check not pitted, rusted or coated with oil)

HT (high tension) or ignition leads and caps (check for dirty, cut, loose, frayed or hard leads

distributor cap (cracks, cleanliness, porosity – examine inside distributor cap for cleanliness generally, and also spark-plug pick-up points)

rotor arm (check not badly scorched or burned out)

distributor cap security clips

contact/breaker unit (not electronic ignition)

distributor shaft

Figure 12 *General ignition system layout*

■■■HOT TIP ■■■■■■■■■

Overheating can cause it to split and leak, signs of which are a high engine temperature reading (needle approaching the red), continuous thick white exhaust smoke, the presence of white mush under the oil filler cap and on the engine oil dipstick, and/or many bubbles in and around the latter; also radiator water that is low or feels oily. You would have to confirm all of these observations before inferring the problem.

Head gasket replacement on the larger, more complex engines (such as V6s) can be very costly due to the difficulty of access to the area.

Steering

Lean through the driver's window while standing outside the car and rotate the steering-wheel from side to side, watching the offside front wheel turning. There should be no visible slack or audible clunking of the steering-wheel – you should notice both road and steering-wheels moving in unison. Many cars come equipped with a steering box (for example, some larger Vauxhalls and BMWs), which comprises many more linkages than a steering rack and so an inch or more of play will be quite acceptable.

Power Steering

A second drive belt will usually tell you that the model is equipped with power steering, and here you are listening for a noisy steering pump, which manifests itself as a bad grumbling or whining sound when the steering-wheel is turned to full lock. Also, when test-driving, the main things to notice are whether the steering appears heavy, moving in uneven jerks or feels as if you are driving on under-inflated tyres. Power steering fluid should be red-coloured (not brown or grey) and up to the mark on its dipstick (a screw cap in the top of the power steering fluid reservoir – see figure 17). It is also worth mentioning that power steering does have an adverse effect on tyre life.

Clutch

You can do a simple test with the clutch to determine whether or not it is slipping. With the engine running *and handbrake on*, depress the clutch and select third or fourth gear (which will put load on the engine) and, with the revs rising only slightly, raise the clutch as if to pull away: if the engine does not stall immediately, then the clutch is slipping. Repeat this test when the engine is warm. More important for the test drive, satisfy yourself that the clutch engages smoothly as you change gear and, particularly on inclines when changing down, note whether the engine revs rise but without an immediate increase in acceleration. This is tell-tale of a slipping clutch. Also when driving there should be no rattling, clonking, juddering or grinding sounds when engaging the clutch.

Alternator

To check that it is passing on charge to the battery, testing is best done in a darkened area, such as inside a garage. With the engine on tick-over and gear lever in neutral, put the lights on to main beam and increase the engine revs. The headlights should become correspondingly brighter as witnessed by the reflection from the wall. With the engine switched off, check too that the alternator fan belt is not slack (see figure 17 and 4.5).

Fan and Water Pump

The cooling system may use a viscous fan coupling (not the electric type of fan) and you will need to test for free play in the fan bearings (particularly if the car has been out of service for some time). With the engine *off*, grab a blade in each hand and try to twist and rock the whole fan assembly back and forth on its spindle: play in the bearings here usually means that a new water pump will soon be needed.

Brakes

If the brakes are servo-assisted (this means that the engine provides help with brake pressure), stand by the open bonnet with the engine running while somebody operates the brake pedal. As the pedal is released, you should not hear any fizzing, hissing or crackling sounds coming from the master cylinder/servo arrangement (see figure 17). A test for brake condition is given in 4.1. The next thing to test is brake effectiveness at both low and high speeds and also during an emergency stop. While on a slope, check the handbrake's holding ability (in an automatic, engage neutral or N when testing the handbrake). Test also the parking brake, P on the automatic gearbox gear shift, and in this case make sure the handbrake is off. Identify and feel the brake pipes underneath the car for corrosion or splits (see figure 10).

Servo Unit

With the engine and handbrake off, pump the brake pedal several times and press the pedal to the floor. Switch the engine on and the brake pedal should dip slightly. This confirms the servo unit is working.

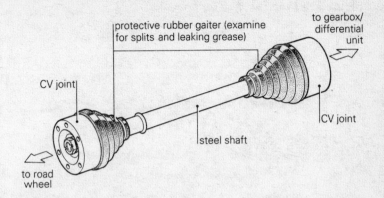

Figure 13a *Drive shaft (also axle shaft or half shaft)*

Drive Shafts

Drive shafts transmit the power to the rear wheels on a rear-wheel-drive car, to the front wheels on a front-wheel-drive car, and to all four wheels on a four-wheel-drive car, from the differentials/gearbox.

Check to see that there are no cracks or splits and no visible grease on the gaiters, which would indicate leaking and therefore a potentially expensive MOT failure (see figure 13a).

Propeller Shafts

The propeller shaft (or prop shaft) runs from the gearbox to the back axle on rear-wheel-drive and to both axles on most four-wheel-drive cars, transmitting power from the engine. Examine the universal joints for wear (or rubber couplings for splits). With excessive wear, you are likely to experience clunking and, eventually, intolerable vibrations that will reduce your speed to a

Figure 13b *Propeller shaft (or prop shaft)*

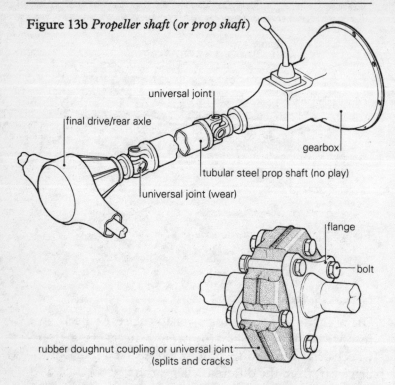

crawl. There should be no play in the shafts at all (see figure 13b).

Exhaust

While a stainless-steel exhaust may last a fair amount of the car's lifetime, those made of mild steel will usually give you only two or three years' service. Every time a car is started from cold, the burning of petrol creates acidic gases, salts and water, which eat at the inside of the exhaust material, and it is for this reason that frequent short journeys corrode an exhaust much more quickly than longer uninterrupted ones. Visibly bad rusting on an exhaust can warrant an MOT failure and

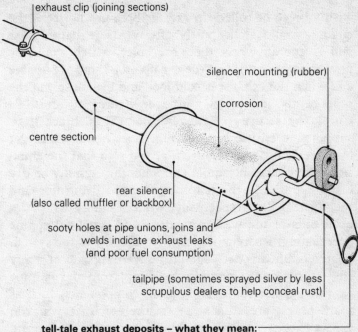

exhaust clip (joining sections)

silencer mounting (rubber)

corrosion

centre section

rear silencer
(also called muffler or backbox)

sooty holes at pipe unions, joins and
welds indicate exhaust leaks
(and poor fuel consumption)

tailpipe (sometimes sprayed silver by less
scrupulous dealers to help conceal rust)

tell-tale exhaust deposits – what they mean:
- black powdery deposits – over-rich fuel mixture, with long-term engine damage
- black gummy deposits – oil burning, wear in pistons, piston rings and cylinders
- white deposits – fuel mixture too weak (can cause ignition problems and overheating)
- water trickle or voluminous white clouds during lengthy test drive – blowing or already blown cylinder head gasket
- rusted tailpipe (while rest of exhaust system in better condition) – plenty of stop-start city driving, bad for long-term engine health

Figure 14 *Schematic of rear section of exhaust system: points to examine*

you will have to make a replacement sooner rather than later. What you will be checking for is that there is at least some life left in the system. A blowing exhaust will seriously increase your fuel consumption. To check for leaks run the engine and cover the exhaust tailpipe tightly with a piece of rolled-up rag: if there are no leaks the engine should stall shortly afterwards (exhaust gases will escape anywhere there are holes, which would by now appear sooty). Get the car up on a ramp if possible and when the exhaust is cold look and feel closely at the pipe bends and metal joins (see figures 10 and 14). Check the security of exhaust mountings, brackets or supports to ensure that the pipe does not rattle or get overstressed as you are driving, and also that the emissions are reasonably quiet and smooth. Gummy or dry black deposits in the tailpipe point to oil burning and fuel system ills, respectively, while a crusty white deposit tells of too weak a mixture and potential engine overheating. Rusty tailpipes (with the rest of the system relatively uncorroded) should be warning you of many cold starts; and a periodic belching from the tailpipe would suggest that worn ignition components, such as spark-plugs, are causing a misfire, or that you can expect expensive valve trouble. Even in the short term, the car will be returning lousy fuel consumption.

A final check to carry out: ensure the boot or tailgate and all windows and air vents are shut, and do sufficiently long a test drive to determine whether you can notice or smell any sign of exhaust emission getting into the cabin, the first indication often being a feeling of drowsiness.

Catalytic Converters

Each new car manufactured from January 1993 needed, by law, to be equipped with a catalytic converter (or cat). The cat is situated at the exhaust manifold (driver's end of the exhaust system) and its job is to reduce the toxicity of emissions, principally carbon monoxide, oxides of nitrogen and unburned hydrocarbons. Some of the more refined catalysts, referred to as three-way cats, are so called because they have the capacity to treat each of these classes of emission individually and with high efficiency.

A catalytic converter will usually come with a one-year manufacturer's warranty, after which a replacement is likely to be expensive. Symptoms of cat malfunction are reported to include rough engine running and subsequent loss in engine power, and also poor starting ability, while the smell of rotten eggs associated with some designs of catalyst can be lessened by simply switching to a brand of unleaded petrol containing a lower sulphur content. Finally, a catalytic converter in poor condition could even fail the car its MOT test if it allows the engine's emissions to exit the tailpipe untreated.

Wheel Bearings

This test is best done with the wheels jacked up, but even if the car is on the road hold each of the front wheels in turn with your hands in a six-o'clock position and rock them backwards and forwards. If you can move them more than about an eighth of an inch you will probably feel a definite click or vibration, which will indicate that the wheel bearings need either adjusting or replacing. During a test drive, you will notice that worn wheel bearings become noisy and contribute vague steering.

Towbar

If a car is already equipped with a towbar this is an indication that the engine may have continually pulled heavy loads – earning itself a punishing mileage into the bargain – and you *must* assume so, particularly if the car's tail-end appears to sag. Conversely, the towbar may have been only recently fitted, or was done so shortly after the car left the factory, yet little used to date. Find out from the previous owner(s) just what has happened; if you intended to use the car for towing or caravanning, the fitting will save you money.

Suspension

A crude yet reasonably effective test for the shock absorbers is the well-known bounce test in which, with the car on level ground, you push down hard on each wing corner in turn. The wing should then rise, dip slightly, rise again, then come to rest. Continued bouncing will mean that your shock absorbers need replacing. An equally telling test is to examine each shock absorber with the car up on a ramp. Visible oil-staining on the damper casings means a leak and therefore loss of efficiency. To maintain the car's proper handling and balance, you need to have them replaced a pair at a time.

Coil Springs

Again, if you can observe the rear springs while standing under a professional hoist, then all the better (see figure 10). If the spring part is actually broken then the car will behave as if there was no spring there at all and, under load, the car will sag, making steering and cornering dangerous. This is both an MOT failure and illegal. Sometimes a coil spring will *settle* with age, reducing its effectiveness. If in doubt use a simple measuring rule to compare their lengths. As with shock absorbers, one ineffective or broken spring is best replaced by a new pair in order to maintain the car's proper handling. And while not an MOT failure in itself, you should check that the springs' rubber mountings are not split. If the car uses leaf springs, again examine them for fractures and also for insecure fixture or excessive sideways movement at their hangers and fixing eyes. Leaf springs may use single or multiple leaves. In either case, examine them for excessive bowing, which is a sign of wear.

Ball Joints and Ball Joint Coverings

These are vital components of the steering/suspension mechanism, which may need renewing if the steering appears sloppy. Even splitting of the rubber coverings would constitute an MOT failure. Check for excess play by lightly grasping the joint while someone turns the steering-wheel. Ball or swivel joints are not normally expensive to replace.

Four-wheel-drive/Off-road-capable Vehicles

While all of the above tests apply equally to four-wheel-drive (4WD) vehicles, there are one or two additional checks you may wish to carry out. Some off-roaders, in particular Land Rovers and Range Rovers, utilize live axles in which the differential gears and drive shafts rotate together inside a single closed casing. Ensure that the axle casing is free from denting and/or other damage due to driving in rough conditions. And while you are underneath the vehicle, inspect a little more thoroughly the condition of the wheels and tyres, underbody, floorings, chassis and cross-members, etc., for the very same reasons – and for corrosion that may have developed as a result. Finally, during the test drive, remember to try out both high- and low-range gears, using the transfer box so as to be sure that you're actually getting four-wheel-drive mode.

Tyres

Tyres make up such an important part of the car's safety that they deserve some extra attention here. First of all, make sure that the car you are looking at has tyres suitable for it (and preferably, but not essentially, all the same brand), since the car's manoeuvring and road-holding characteristics will depend on this. Check the details as in figure 15.

Condition

An interesting fact is that almost a quarter of MOT failures are due at least in part to worn or damaged tyres (*Which?* magazine, April 1990), so you should check their condition from the outset. The handbook will tell you the correct pressures for both laden and unladen states under headings of Specifications, Forecourt Information or Steering and Suspension. It is a good idea also to buy yourself a tyre-pressure and tread-depth gauge (which you can get from somewhere like Halfords for around £6 for the two). If you find the pressures incorrect you should wonder why; after all, the current owner may not care very much now but it will be you who forks out for a set of replacements if they have been neglected. Check that there is in fact a spare in the back, check its pressure and that it is not worn, flat or damaged, and, most important, that it matches the other tyres in size and both width and bias (see figure 15). Then locate the wheel jack and brace, ensuring their compatability with both wheel nuts and jacking points. Next, look at the rear tyres end-on, noticing if any bulges here are due to the weight of the car and not an irregularity. To check this, move the car forward a few inches and check that bulging remains in the same position above the ground as before. Look at each of the tyre sidewalls in turn, checking for cracks, splits, cuts and evidence of kerbing, in which the tyres have been scraped along the kerbside when parking (often the wheel rims and covers will be scratched in sympathy). If you find this on a model with power steering then you will have greater reason to want to check the wheel balancing and alignment (see later). Some tyres, even budget ones, have a kerb ridge – a 3mm x 3mm rubber protrusion around the middle of the tyre sidewall, specially incorporated to protect against damaging the tyre wall when kerbing. You should also expect the tyre grooves to be free of bits of glass, stones and other road debris, clean, and for all the valve caps to be in place. Anyone who has looked after their tyres will have periodically seen to this; in fact the general condition of the tyres is a good indication of how the car has been treated in its more recent past (see figure 10).

Tread Wear
The legal minimum requirement for the depth of tyre tread is currently 1.6mm across the central three quarters of the tread pattern with at least visible tread over the remainder. Many tyres today contain tread wear indicators (TWIs, see figure 15), rubber inserts which, when visible on the tyre surface, will be telling you that your treads are right down to the very legal limit. They found much more useful application as a warning when our legal tread limits were set at 1mm.

Next use your tread-depth gauge over various points of the tread pattern and note any irregularities such as excessive wearing at the tyre edges (due to possible under-inflation) or excessive wear at the centre of the tread (due to over-inflation). Check for uneven wear on any tyre, which could be caused by anything from out-of-balance wheels or worn shock absorbers to a serious steering defect (which could be very expensive to put right). In such cases the owner might have swapped the back wheels for the front in an attempt to disguise the problem.

Ageing
Cracks and splits on tyre walls, while giving an indication of how the car has been driven, can also tell you whether it has been active or idle for any length of time. Tyres on a car that has been sitting around for many months may have been seriously weakened in structure from inactivity and sunlight, making them dangerous to drive on. Look for other signs too – dust on and under the bonnet, black imprints left by the front tyres, long-term oil-stained pavements and, if applicable, grass that has yellowed underneath the bodywork. Do not be afraid to ask questions about any aspect of the car's history.

Load and Speed Specifications
Another thing your handbook will tell you is the maximum speed and load specifications of the tyres for that model. True, for a fifteen-year-old banger that you intend to use only locally, performance tyres are not going to be a priority. However, for a more recent model in which you intend to carry heavy luggage repeatedly over long distances, then tyre suitability becomes much more critical. You can glean valuable information from the sidewall of a tyre and one of the most important factors is the speed/load capacity. The sidewall coding tells you the tyre's maximum speed and maximum load. Figure 15 shows a fairly typical tyre sidewall and also what the relevant information displayed there means. The tables in figure 15 refer to the

most commonly occurring range of speed and load ratings for tyres, which you can check with your handbook.

Figure 15 *Tyre sidewall information*

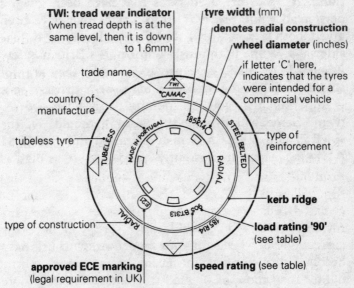

load and speed rating tables

speed rating symbol	L	M	N	P	Q	R	S	T	U	H	V	Z
maximum speed for which tyre is capable (mph)	75	81	87	95	100	105	113	118	125	130	150	over 150

load rating	60	70	80	90	100	110
load (kg)	250	335	450	600	800	1060

Retreads and Remoulds

There are some differences of opinion among tyre dealers over the distinction between retreads and remoulds,
with some even saying that they are one and the same
thing. *Retreads* are used tyres that have been given a
new tread while *remoulds* are old tyres that have been
given both a new tread and renewed rubber on the
sidewalls. While both must conform to a British Safety
Standard (to enable safe use at 70 mph) they are not
actually suitable for continued high-speed driving, so it
is important that you can identify them when you see
them. Some will display the word 'remould' on the
sidewall and others a British Standard number (BSI
AU144b). Many are currently speed-rated to as high as
95mph.

Wheel Types

As with tyres, you should make sure you have the
correct *type* of wheels for your model. Alloy wheels have
become very popular in recent years, being a little
lighter than those of pressed steel and somewhat more
stylish. Alloys damage quite easily though: kerbing and
corrosion by road salt and brake dust will quickly lead
to their having to be re-lacquered.

Which Model?

If you are buying a top-of-the-range model then the
chances are you will know exactly which wheel trims
you should be getting for your money. However, when
buying something like a GL model (or any model that
is one of a whole family of trim levels), you could end up
with L trims if the seller thinks he can get away with it.
It is a peculiar thing that people often rate their cars
according to extras and refinements and so inadvertently

buying the wrong ones now might even affect your asking price at resale time.

Balancing and Tracking

If you are not sure whether the wheels have been recently balanced and properly aligned, you should see to it now (see chapter 9). Neither have anything to do with normal servicing but by getting the job done now you could help save yourself literally hundreds of pounds in premature tyre replacement and exorbitant fuel bills. Wheels that are out of balance will cause noticeable steering-wheel shake upon acceleration at between 40–60 mph and will grip the road with less efficiency, with the result that you will rapidly and unevenly wear your tyres. Tracking (front-wheel alignment), on the other hand, ensures your front wheels are

Figure 16 *Feathering caused by poor wheel alignment (outside tyre-tread portion affected)*

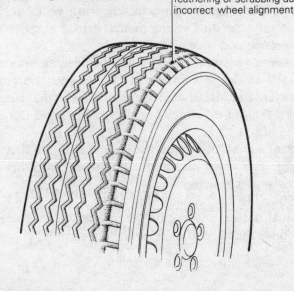

feathering or scrubbing due to incorrect wheel alignment

angled correctly and therefore that they are running in their truly intended path. If not, you will be wasting more fuel, unevenly wearing your tyres and also affecting the suspension and steering characteristics of your car. Examine the outside edges of the tyres for feathering as evidence of poor wheel alignment (see figure 16).

3.3 Diesel Cars

In chapter 1 we touched briefly upon the case for diesel ownership and, although much the same structural and mechanical testing criteria can be applied to both petrol- and diesel-engined models, it is worth noting additionally that diesels can be particularly expensive to repair. Be sure to look and listen out for the following:

- Tough life: better fuel consumption, durability and high resale potential could mean the car has enjoyed a hard life as a taxi or similar workhorse. Be especially vigilant then for prematurely worn upholstery, carpet and trim on a young model, drilled bumper(s) and interior and very high mileage
- Full service history: there should be adequate documentary evidence to support the frequent engine oil, filter and diesel-fuel filter changes (the latter every 5,000 miles) which are essential to good (long) engine life
- Voluminous black exhaust smoke and sluggish drive: it suggests a worn distributor pump and injectors – expensive to replace
- Serious oil leaks and bad cold starts
- Unusual noises: any out-of-the ordinary clatter over and above the normal diesel warm-up sounds.

4 Test-driving a Used Car

Introduction

Test-driving a car that you intend keeping for a good few years is essential and I would recommend at least an hour for this. You do need time to understand the new proposition and, after all, what is an hour spent now compared to ownership of three years or more? In test-driving you will not only be deciding if this is the next car for you but will also be weighing up one figure – the asking price set by the dealer or seller – against another figure – the cost of anything that might need replacing. You should be prepared to negotiate at least something and the seller will be expecting it (even those who appear to have precluded offers from their price!). Make at least mental notes of the things that will need attention and discuss them with the dealer or seller *now*, since not only will the nuisance factor be multiplied later but, if you accept the car in its present condition, it may prove very difficult to get assistance with recurring faults after the sale (see 6.3).

By test-driving you are demonstrating much interest in buying the car and this is a good enough reason to warrant spending the time doing so. As a buyer you may feel a certain obligation or pressure to buy for fear of wasting the seller's time – particularly when you've already spent an hour inspecting the mechanicals. However, do resist the temptation to buy the first car you look at (unless it really is up to scratch). Remember: no promises have been made to the seller. If you *do* experience dealer (or seller) pressure one way to relieve it may be to explain – preferably on the phone beforehand – that you'll need some time to examine the car properly since you'll be buying it to drive to and around, for example, Russia, and that once there the vehicle will be subject to a very thorough overhaul before the authorities will even let you in. Almost without exception this method has bought me much valuable time. And what about rejecting a car that you'd not be happy to buy – how to tell the seller face to face? The key is simply always to give yourself a way out: tell the seller you'll 'be back when you've seen the other car in West Street later today . . .'. Don't confuse this with time-wasting, it's just a means of giving yourself some extra thinking time should you need it. And besides, the seller's feelings remain intact when you call later.

Some of the following is probably going to sound obvious, and you could claim that any person can decide these things for themselves. But beware – it is easy to fall in love with a car, to decide to buy it even before you've test-driven it, and then lower your standard of expectation to fit that particular example.

▰▰ Preliminary Checks

Before you drive the car, there are a number of preliminary checks that you will need to carry out to decide if the car is going to be suitable. Before test-driving, take another good look at the car's overall appearance by walking around it once more to satisfy yourself that you can live with any scratches, dents, surface rust, slight paint mismatches, a tear in the vinyl hood or a dented bumper: if you cannot now, then you won't be able to afterwards.

Comfort and Visibility

After taking in the size, shape and appearance of the car, get in and note *how* you sit in the driver's seat. For example, does the seat sag? Are you sitting high enough? And do you have sufficient leg-room? Can you reach the gear lever and steering-wheel comfortably? What about your view through the windscreen? Is it improved with respect to your current car or do the windscreen pillars obstruct your vision of oncoming and side-turning traffic? When you look out of the side windows do you have to crook your neck or twist your shoulder to do so? And then the view out of the rear window – you will have to test reverse gear sooner or later. Check now that you are the right build for the car and that when reversing your vision will not be obstructed by a tall headrest or a too-acutely sloping rear windscreen. When adjusting the seat, consider whether it will interfere with your passengers; for example, whether you will have to endure their knees in your back or whether you would have to teach them some pretty advanced yoga positions before you will let them ride with you again! You can test their available leg-room by adjusting the driver's seat to your liking and then getting into the back seat. Check also that these do not sag at all. These are important points. Seat security is also now an MOT testable item. Check if the driver's seat has any kind of lumbar adjustment – a lever or extra cog-wheel arrangement on the side of the seat – and, if so, does it make any difference? Put on the seat-belt and check that it is not badly frayed at the sides – an MOT failure – and do the same check on the front (and any other) passenger belt(s). Satisfy yourself that the seat-belts pull well, do not stick (or take for ever to return to their rest positions, therefore hinting at a probable high-mileage car) and also that their anchorage points are secure. If not, then on some cars this could point to a rusted sill. If anything bothers you, note it.

Engine and Brakes

Ideally, you will have already made the checks in chapter 3. If not, at least give yourself the chance to open the bonnet, start the engine and watch what happens. Your handbook would have made you familiar with the location of the most important engine-bay components and you should try to identify at least some of the more obvious ones (see figure 17).

Check there is nothing seriously amiss and note the cleanness of the engine which, if not specially steam cleaned, will give you a fair indication of its life during previous ownership.

Next, go back to the driver's seat and prepare to do a test on the brakes: switch the engine on first and then depress the brake pedal in one deliberate movement to the point where it will not go any further. The pedal should stay put – if it drops further to the floor pan (a leak), or softens underfoot (air in the system), then it is not in a very healthy condition and will be a major point for you to negotiate. This, then, has tested the (hydraulic) brake pressure and is the first test of brake effectiveness.

The next test is designed to measure the state of wear of the engine – we've all followed cars that show signs of serious wear, belching out thick black or blue clouds though the exhaust. Black exhaust, as previously mentioned, indicates too rich a mixture and that you are wasting petrol (check you have returned the choke!) or that you will need to replace your air filter, while

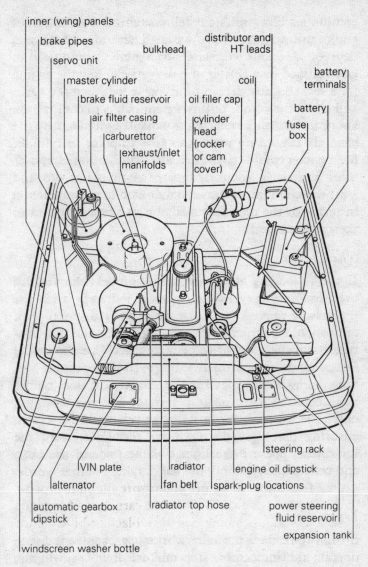

inner (wing) panels

brake pipes

bulkhead

servo unit

distributor and HT leads

master cylinder

coil

battery terminals

brake fluid reservoir

oil filler cap

battery

air filter casing

cylinder head (rocker or cam cover)

fuse box

carburettor

exhaust/inlet manifolds

steering rack

VIN plate

radiator

engine oil dipstick

alternator

fan belt

spark-plug locations

automatic gearbox dipstick

radiator top hose

power steering fluid reservoir

expansion tank

windscreen washer bottle

Figure 17 *Engine bay: some of the more common under-bonnet components*

continuous blue emissions tell you that the valve guides and/or piston rings have worn. There are, of course, degrees of serious wear and a *bad* engine would need to be identified by a cluster of observations. Rev the engine for a few seconds, return to idling speed, then rev again and check the colour of further emissions to confirm the above tests. Continuous white exhaust emissions, by the way, are caused by water vapour and point to cylinder head gasket trouble, which, as already mentioned, can be more serious in some designs of engine (the V6s and V8s) than in others (four-cylinder in-line arrangements) in terms of the amount of labour and cost involved in their replacement.

The Controls

If you're looking at a more deluxe model than you are used to, it is very easy to get carried away with the impressive range of extras now at your disposal. Not only should you familiarize yourself with the new features (and there ought to be a handbook for the model in the glove compartment), but for safety reasons you must know where eveything is and what it does before you decide to drive off. Go through the gear changes, check the windscreen wipers when you wash the screen, ensuring that they do not leave tramlines, work the indicators, operate the light switches, sound the horn and release then reapply the handbrake: in other words, get the feel of the car before you take it out on the road.

Lights

So that you can see the lights working, get someone else to operate the indicators, stop and tail-lights, sidelights, main beam and dipped-light action (also, fog and driving lights where applicable). All should be working properly and failure to do so may constitute an MOT failure (remember: if more than just a bulb has gone their remedy may be costly, so now is the time to negotiate). Indicators should tick at the right speed and should not be temperamental. It is also an offence to drive the car if the indicators or brake lights are not working. You may need to start the engine to operate the reversing lights, if fitted – inadequate indication to traffic behind you of your intention to reverse could be potentially very dangerous. Remember to check that the door-opening courtesy light and any strategically placed map-reading lights work. When you get a chance, pull into a shaded area and determine that the dashboard panel can be sufficiently illuminated.

At this stage, note again the feel of the driver's seat and how your back feels. If you really cannot get comfortable in the seat now, then think hard about whether you really want to go any further with this car. Anything that irritates you now will annoy you ten times as much later, so remember there is no obligation to accept anything you do not like during the test drive.

Insurance Cover

A final point before you drive away is to check that you are in fact covered to drive the car – often only third-party cover will be necessary.

◼ HOT TIP ◼

Often, but not always, a dealer will arrange this for the purpose of a short drive, but privately this will not be the case. The unexpected can and does happen, particularly in an unfamiliar car, and even if it is not your fault who is going to pay for any resulting damage? It could cost you even more than the asking price of the car if there is bad damage, so do be sure about this point.

4.2 The Drive

After checking again that the tyres are properly inflated,
and having adjusted the rear-view and door mirrors as
necessary, assume a relaxed posture, slowly move off
and drive around for at least ten minutes while you get
used to the car's handling characteristics. Try to find a
mix of roads, busy junctions as well as quiet lanes, and
if you do not know the area well ask the seller to let you
explore as many different roads as possible. After driving for a while you will be better able to appreciate
what the car can offer you and this will be a good basis
for any subsequent judgements you make. Once you
have got used to the controls, slow down and stop the
car to see if it brakes in a straight line or whether it
pulls to one side. If it does pull you may be looking at
an expensive remedy since this could be due to badly
bedded brake pads (although brake pads themselves
are fairly cheap to replace) a sticky caliper or warped
front brake discs (often accompanied by a noticeable
steering-wheel wobble). Listen out for any squealing or
screeching noises which could be dust on the brake
linings (normally rear brakes), indicating the need for
servicing, or maybe badly worn brake pads and discs
that will need replacing. (In such cases you will have
suspected this already when you tested the brake pedal.)
Also heed any available dashboard warning lights for
confirmation that the brakes need renewing or that
hydraulic brake fluid is leaking.

Anti-lock Brakes (ABS)

Testing for anti-lock brakes should be done in the same
way, the main difference being that you will experience underfoot a pulsating pedal – a normal condition

of their operation. ABS is a relatively recent item whose faults appear to be more electrical than mechanical so you should satisfy yourself of the good working order of the dashboard warning lights. An important point is that while the anti-lock feature is additional to the basic braking facility, failure of any part of it will mean (perhaps expensive) failure of the MOT test.

Transmission

If the car has manual transmission, note if the clutch grabs or whether you can confirm that it is slipping (see 3.2). Make sure you test all of the gears in turn, which will mean having to find a long stretch of road where you can build up a reasonable speed. Do not forget to test reverse gear. Note any noises that do not sound good and be satisfied that the gearbox responds properly to up-and-down changing without any accompanying crunching noises (worn synchromesh). In particular, try moving from fourth or third gear down to second – if it requires unreasonable effort now then you can be sure that it won't improve with use. Once you've accelerated comfortably into each gear, take your foot off the accelerator pedal and be warned if the gear lever jumps into neutral: it means a worn gearbox mechanism and that you'll be needing a new or reconditioned gearbox.

With automatics, gear changes should feel smooth, quiet and relatively jerk-free. Selecting drive (D) or reverse (R) via neutral (N) should not be noisy or take longer than a couple of seconds. If it does, it could mean a costly replacement, while jolting or hiccuping at the regular change-up speeds, or indeed sluggish acceleration, probably points to the automatic gearbox fluid being low or that it has been for some time.

As with a slipping clutch or any other faulty component estimate, if you can, what the replacement and
its fitting is likely to cost and whether this refers to
new, reconditioned or second-hand parts. This is not
always easy to do accurately, but the more plausible
the figures that you can come up with the more the
seller will believe you know what you're talking about
and the easier the negotiation will be. If you don't want
to take the risk don't buy the car. Find one in better
condition.

Handling and Performance

Compare the general handling of the car with your
present one, noting how this car copes with corners and
road defects like potholes. You will have done the crude
shock absorber test while the car was stationary. This
time notice the extent to which road bumps are absorbed
when you drive over them. Does the suspension wallow
as you take corners? And at higher speeds, 40–60 mph,
what happens when you take your foot off the accelerator? Do you get a characteristic clonking noise? This
could indicate that either your propeller shaft(s) or your
differential unit is in trouble, whereas a clicking or
clonking upon acceleration or tight cornering can be
indicative of badly wearing drive shafts. And if the
model is turbo-charged, does it deliver the extra power
(boost pressure) on demand? If not, and if there is any
shrill whistling in conjunction with heavy oil consumption, this will be an indication of imminent turbo
failure.

Do listen carefully to any unusual or repetitive noises
and try to match them with likely symptoms you might
have read about (and gone on to investigate) from previous sections in this book.

■ **HOT TIP** ▬▬▬▬▬▬▬▬▬▬

When in doubt about expensive-sounding noises – do not accept reassurances or the car.

Steering

Note any vibrations in the steering-wheel: shaking that starts at around 40–55 mph indicates wheels out of balance, whereas excess play in the steering-wheel can be a sign of steering mechanism wear. Back this up by examining the front tyres for excessive tread wear particularly at the tyre edges. Marked veering towards the kerb or towards the centre of the road on an otherwise straight flat road points to poor wheel alignment. If you have the time and can get to a good tyre specialist request a few quick alignment checks; if they refuse to do the tracking for you because of some significant steering fault, then either ask the seller or dealer to put it right, having announced your findings, or, failing that, simply forget the car. Steering defects can be expensive to put right.

Air-conditioning

Air-conditioning really only finds application in this country for a few weeks at most and so is still considered something of a luxury item. It is an option that seldom holds its value in any used car.

When using air-conditioning there may be an initial delay of several seconds – however, you need to beware of intermittent operation or the system blowing insufficiently cool air. Air-conditioning requires regular and fairly expensive charging, it increases fuel consumption and, in an older car, is likely to be less reliable and hence all the more costly if needing repair. It may be a luxury you can do without.

Noise (and Smell)

This is very important to assess since it is derived from different sources. Make sure the radio-cassette is turned off, wind the windows up and turn off heater fans. An unfamiliar-sounding engine, even if quieter than your present car, will still contribute some noise. Other noises will come from any of the body panels that are capable of rattling, such as doors or the boot, or from mechanical components such as exhausts, wheel bearings or axles, and you should be able to distinguish between these and other noises caused by such things as wheel jacks, spare tyres or tools that are thrown about while the car is in motion. Road noise from tyres is the other main contribution and, combined, all these sources will have a telling effect on your driving (how long and for what general purpose are your journeys likely to be?). Treat any irregular grinding, clunking or rasping noises as definitely *not* normal. A long test drive is essential to determine what level of normal noise is tolerable to you.

Note any irregular smells that arise during the course of the test drive – these might include burning of rubber and oil or the leaking of petrol or exhaust fumes, and are extra points that you may use as a lever in your negotiations.

Gauge Indicators

Speedometer

Check that the speedometer is properly responsive and that the needle is not erratic (see 2.3). It may be accurate to within 10 per cent. At the same time satisfy yourself that both the odometer and trip counter display are actually working in step – and you should note, on paper if necessary, the mileages of both before the drive.

Fuel Gauge

Don't be afraid to put in a couple of gallons, especially if you are going to spend a while test-driving. For one thing, you will be able to check that the gauge needle actually rises to a new level when you fill up (fuel gauges are not cheap to fix) and also that it falls with consumption, giving you at least an idea of the model's efficiency. Do remember that even if you don't buy this particular car you are still investing valuably in the one that you eventually do.

Oil Pressure Gauge

Some of the more luxurious models come equipped with an oil gauge but you will need to know that a reading is meaningful. Rely more on what the manual and handbook tell you rather than on the dealer or seller. Remember also the value of talking with friends or colleagues or in fact with anyone who owns a similar model to the one you are thinking of buying. Better to know now, for example, whether you should expect a characteristically low oil pressure reading for this type (and age) of car or whether, in conjunction with other observations, you might be unearthing clues to an otherwise tired engine.

Engine Temperature Gauge

Ensure the engine temperature gauge is properly responsive. If a test drive produces no reading at all, it could be traceable to little more than a blown temperature switch (£3), or maybe something far more sinister such

Figure 18 *Engine temperature gauge in the red*

as the owner having removed the thermostat in order to disguise a persistent overheating problem.

Battery Meter

In models equipped with a battery meter, note that the needle should be reading just into the positive sector (see figure 19) – assuming no other electrics are being used, for example, radio, lights, windscreen wipers, interior lights, etc.

Figure 19 *A typical battery meter*

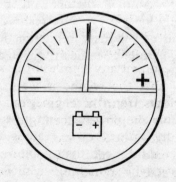

4.3 Know Your Model

Never underestimate the value of having spoken with people owning like models. Usually they will be quite honest and ready to talk at length about their cars. They will probably be able to tell you all about the car's quirks and any peculiarities they have experienced (as well as its general running costs) and, of course, knowing about these things beforehand is going to put you in a much more objective frame of mind if and when these acceptable anomalies manifest themselves.

4.4 Leaks Tests

Test-drive long enough to allow the engine to properly warm up, thereby allowing time for any serious faults to emerge – for example, thick oil additives will subsequently thin out and therefore reveal the knocking, rattling or other mechanical ills they were put there to disguise in the first instance.

After about forty-five minutes (twenty-five if hurried) or at the end of the test drive, you should park the car over a reasonably clean, dry paving stone or a similar stretch of driveway. The purpose of leaving it parked like this for about ten to fifteen minutes (and you could be examining the manual, brushing up on the controls, reading the service history or even chatting to the seller in this time) is so that any significant leaks will start to show up now that the engine is warm. You will be watching for leaks from the engine, radiator, gearbox, axle and possibly the power steering reservoir. Bear in mind that though a little oil can go a long way, even small drops could be hiding something much more serious if neglected – remember, you do not actually know how long any developing problem has persisted for. At the end of the fifteen minutes, look for the likely sources of any leaks (identifying them by colour in the case of distinguishing red automatic gearbox fluid from black or brown engine oil).

4.5 Under-bonnet Checks

At the end of the test-drive, and with the engine still warm, restart it and take another look under the bonnet (see figure 17). Any checks now should either confirm or allay any fears of problems you might have suspected. BE CAREFUL NOT TO SCALD YOUR HAND ON THE RADIATOR CAP AND KEEP YOUR HANDS WELL CLEAR OF ALL POTEN- TIALLY DANGEROUS MOVING PARTS. Firstly check for oil escape. Although engines ought to be oil-tight systems, older ones and especially those worn or abused tend to allow some oil out. Look at the oil filler cap (see figure 17), breather valves and engine oil dipstick for oil vapour escaping under pressure. This still may not indicate a particularly bad engine but if you have also observed a consistently low oil pressure reading in conjunction with thick blue and/or white exhaust clouds, then you might, understandably, be reluctant to buy this car (see 3.2). Still with the engine running, and selector in P, pull the transmission oil dipstick* (see figure 17) and read the level in the same way you would the engine oil. The fluid should be red, *not* orange or brown, and should not smell burned. If it does, expect a very expensive bill for a new torque converter – equivalent to a clutch in an

*Automatics only.

automatic – and gearbox overhaul. Also at this time, glance around the engine bay for signs of bodged workmanship – rounded bolt tops or forced, chewed, burred or worn screw heads, etc.

Fan Belts

Inspect the drive belts while they are stationary to confirm any fraying or cracking. Check the tension on the belt by trying to twist the underside right round (you should not be able to if the tension is correct). On more deluxe models and especially on those with larger engines you will see two if not three belts. The second will be for the power steering and the third for the air-conditioning. A slipping fan belt will make a continuous screeching or whistling noise. They are cheap enough to adjust or replace.

Radiator Leaks

You will have noted both the colour and level of the radiator water before the test drive, when the radiator was cold. You should not have to refill a radiator except occasionally (and in sealed systems hardly ever); when the radiator cap has cooled down sufficiently, check that the water level has not appreciably dropped. If it has, then consider other factors: was the engine temperature reading high? (in which case you could have a blocked or leaking radiator, a defective thermostat, or head gasket trouble). Did you get a consistently white exhaust emission? Check the general state of the radiator fins for areas of damage and also under the car for evidence of leaking water; check the radiator-to-engine bottom hose. Check again for the presence of bubbles on the engine oil dipstick along with any white mushy precipitate (water and oil), both of which suggest cylinder head gasket problems. At the same time check that the oil is both reasonably clean and up to the mark on the dipstick (wipe the dipstick clean, reinsert and then remove and read again to obtain a meaningful measurement).

Radiator Hoses

Unless obviously repaired with tape, the radiator hoses will appear to be in good order when cold. The top hose is the one that gets the hottest and is most likely to burst; however, examine its shape some forty-five minutes after driving. A large bulge could burst at any time and continued driving (about thirty minutes) could be sufficient to wreck your engine. Hoses are not actually very expensive, not more than about £3–£4, but you should negotiate a discount on anything that seems a potential problem; for example, brittle or perished rubber. Remember, too, that repaired hoses should be treated as temporary and would need replacing at the first opportunity.

4.6 Other Points to Watch

Electronic Warning Lights

Electronic warning lights have become increasingly common in later cars and indeed serve a very useful function. The display can be anywhere on the dashboard but can also be overhead, near the rear-view mirror. The lights warn of problems like fuel shortage, front brake pads wearing thin, low engine coolant level, low engine oil level and possibly low windscreen washer fluid level. When you start the engine they all come on and then one by one go out when the fault that they are there to indicate is not apparent. Sometimes, however, the fuel shortage warning lights flash on even though there is still over half a tank of fuel; or although new brake pads have been fitted recently the appropriate warning light still comes on. In these cases you will need to have the wiring examined. This could be evidence of former collision damage in which the panel around which the wiring was arranged has been knocked, upsetting the necessary circuitry providing the warning. The cost of putting this right can run into several hundreds of pounds so you will need to be sure that this warning system is very definitely what you need, or that you can live with faulty warnings in the first place. You should also check for any bulbs that have been removed or need replacing and that no wires are frayed or are in contact with any other wires or components relating to other applications.

Fuel Cap

If you have enough fuel in the tank for the test-drive you will probably not even think to examine the cap. Do ensure that you have the right one. It has even been known for buyers to find only a rolled-up piece of rag in the tank neck! The fuel cap now constitues a part of the MOT test and so even the temporary push-in-pull-out type with plastic fins will fail the car the test if it doesn't actually seal the filler neck. Also, beware the lockable types of cap that appear to jump off the moment you undo them since they are almost certainly the wrong ones and you risk putting the tank under too much pressure if it cannot breathe properly.

Draughts, Window Winders and Sun-roofs

Unless you have a passenger with you, it is unlikely that you will have noticed draughts coming from anywhere but the driver's window or door. Check the operation of all (electric) window lifts and that all windows open and close properly, with ease. The same goes for the sun-roof – make sure you know its modes of action; for example, sliding and/or tilting, and that it is not unduly stiff. Cars have been sold with the sun-roof deliberately *not* advertised, and when the buyer got home, he realized why. Check too the operation of the (electric) aerial. If it doesn't extend/retract satisfactorily you'll need to budget to at least £40 for repairs. Remember to try out the heater and ventilation controls, ensuring that they're in working order.

Windscreen Cracks and Mirrors

Windscreen chips are easy to overlook since they are not always obvious and you are not actually looking for them when driving.

◼◼ HOT TIP ◼◼

Recent MOT legislation demands that windscreens be completely free of cracks that could impair the driver's line of vision. Be wary of any strategically placed tax discs or stickers to conceal glass disfigurements and, finally, note that both interior and exterior rear-view mirrors will only pass the MOT if in good condition, free of cracks and fully adjustable.

Check Dimensions

Lastly, if you are buying a longer or wider car than your present one and you have a garage or fairly narrow driveway in which to park, it would be sensible, if test-driving near home, to arrange to drive it for size – check you can manoeuvre the car in and out without a squeeze.

If you cannot take the car home, then look in the handbook for the length and width dimensions, having previously measured your driveway or garage.

Two or Three Models

Having got the feel of this model, you will have a pretty good idea of whether or not you want to buy it. My advice is that even if you are very keen, you should definitely take the time to test another, or even two more of the same model in similar price ranges. No two models are exactly the same, even if identical in age, trim level, engine capacity and mileage, and in test-driving them you could feel a world of difference in the way that each of the cars handle and respond. Even your instinctive feelings towards them can vary. You should never assume that simply because one car is priced higher than another that it is necessarily going to be the better buy. When buying privately it is not always possible to hold a car over for you, because the vendor will want to sell immediately to the first person willing to put up the cash. This is why I suggest you choose to test-drive from a dealer first, in which case the car will probably still be on the forecourt in a few days' time.

5 Getting Extra Help in Choosing the Right Car – Vehicle Inspections

■ Introduction

You should now feel more confident about judging the mechanical and structural soundness of a used car, but there can still be no substitute for a second opinion – a valued opinion from a qualified person, that is. Some of the best professional help can take the form of a vehicle inspection service, in which a member of a motoring organization, or other skilled mechanic, will examine your prospective vehicle and perhaps notice some extra things not immediately obvious to the layman (for example, the increasingly common phenomenon of the cut-and-shut repair, in which a badly accident-damaged vehicle is inadequately reconstructed from two halves of completely different cars).

Services here can be comprehensive but should include all the points discussed in previous chapters. (See also figures 24a, b and c.)

5.1 Motoring Organizations

The AA charges according to type of car. Inspections of smaller cars (which they class as group 1) cost £90 for members and £106 for non-members. For larger cars (group 2) the cost is £100 for members, £120 for non-members. These sums may seem large, but the inspection *could* save you from making an expensive mistake on an already expensively priced vehicle.

The examination typically lasts two hours and you can expect something like a six-page report summarizing the car's overall condition, opinions on what might have to be put right, the good points and whether or not the asking price is fair.

For safety reasons, a car sold privately would have to be examined in a place off the road and you should make sure beforehand that it carries a valid MOT certificate.

A disadvantage of the system is that waiting time can be as long as three to five days, and you could wait a further two days to receive the report. Cars on dealers' forecourts may well remain available for that length of time, but those advertised privately often sell the very same day. If you can pay by credit card, this might help reduce the waiting period.

The RAC offers the same kind of service, which comprises visual inspection, road test and detailed report. Waiting time is again in the order of three to five days and you need not be an RAC member to use the service (but, irrespective of vehicle, you will be charged an extra premium). Prices start at around £90 for engines of 2.499 litres and under; over 2.5 litres starting at £100 and higher-performance cars such as Jaguars, Jensens and some BMWs at £200 or more.

National Breakdown no longer do inspections of used cars.

Contract Inspections

The AA and RAC also engages in contract inspections for garages; any examined car displays a sticker (red tick with AA motif) on its windscreen (or 'Supercheck'

stickers in the case of Austin Rover garages or RAC
'Motorscan' in the case of Ford dealers). Ask at the
garage for the accompanying report, which should be
available on request.

5.2 Private Inspections

There are several other equally valuable inspection
services you might consider that can work out cheaper.
The service is usually offered by mechanics either as
spare-time business or as an extension to their regular
work. You can find local mechanics advertising this
service in weekly newspapers.

When choosing an inspection service try not to be
guided by price alone. You may have to pay a little
more for a good mechanic who does a thorough job.
When making telephone inquiries, be sure to ask some
of the following questions in order to distinguish the
amateur enthusiasts from the genuine and experienced.
Ask:

- How long he's been doing inspections, if he is a
  qualified mechanic, and also how many inspections
  he usually does in a month, say
- What kind of tools and equipment he intends to
  bring with him (for testing a battery or alternator
  perhaps; for removing spark-plugs; checking for
  cooling system leaks or, indeed, for conducting
  a cylinder-compression test)
- What you can expect for your money – will the
  examination take one or two hours or more? Will
  you get some kind of written assessment afterwards,
  and if not then what do you get?

- Exactly how much an all-in inspection will cost. Some could offer inspections *from* £X where X might relate to a basic mini model. Ask if he will actually examine your model – and remember to ask how he wants to be paid, for example, in cash only or by cheque with a guarantee card
- If it doesn't already state it in the advert, confirm that his territorial limits do cover the area your car is in – there is little point in getting quotes, discussing practice, making arrangements, etc., only to find that he does not cover your area
- Ask if the inspector intends advising you as to the worth of the car at the end of the examination, or indeed if he will do some of the negotiating with the seller on your behalf. This is going to be particularly important if you are not conversant with the prices of spares. After all, the fact that you will need a new clutch, offside front tyre, front brake pads, wheel bearing adjustment and new exhaust back-box is not going to mean much if you don't know the cost of the replacements on this particular car. (This also illustrates the value of using a working mechanic, who should be able to estimate prices of parts to within a good 5 per cent or 10 per cent either way.) Some inspectors are only concerned with the car's general condition and roadworthiness, but then leave the negotiations with the dealer or seller to you. Find out what he is prepared to do, *beforehand*
- Ask the *seller* beforehand if you can bring along a vehicle inspector to help you, since not all sellers will welcome a professional's opinion. Inviting someone along unannounced might not only waste everyone's time if you are not allowed to go ahead with the inspection, but will mean you'll probably still have

to pay the inspector at least a minimum call-out charge

- Lastly, if at all possible, try to look at the vehicle yourself *before* you enlist the help of an inspector. You will have done this for a car sitting on a dealer's forecourt, but for a car advertised privately this is more difficult. The value of a quick preview is to help you decide whether or not you want to go any further with the model. You may discover that it is the wrong colour, has suffered crash damage, is of quite a different specification, etc. – and you do not want to pay for an inspection on a car that you are now no longer interested in.

◼◼ HOT TIP ◼◼

You might also consider asking to drive the car to an MOT testing station (not the one that tested the car most recently) – preferably one operated by a main dealer of that particular make of car where, for a small charge, they can look the vehicle over for you. Such places do not always have repair facilities and, since they are not necessarily soliciting business, will be more likely to offer an impartial opinion on any work that might need to be carried out.

6 Guarantees, Warranties and Your Basic Legal Rights

6.1 A Code of Practice for the Used-car Trade

The Society of Motor Manufacturers and Traders (SMMT), the Retail Motor Industry Federation (RMIF, formerly the Motor Agents' Association, MAA), and the Scottish Motor Trade Association (SMTA) in conjunction with the Office of Fair Trading, have set up a code of practice outlining the basic standards you should expect from (used-) car dealers in general, but which in practice obliges only members belonging to their respective associations.

The value of being familiar with this is obvious since if you know – and can demonstrate that you know – the obligations a dealer has to you, then at the very least you can expect better treatment (if not also a better price!). You could also challenge non-member garages since their trading should follow similar lines. Within the code of practice at least the following must be observed:

- The Sale of Goods Act: among other things, this prohibits misleading descriptions (see below)
- Inspection facilities: these must be adequate to enable you to inspect a car to a reasonable level of thoroughness

- Documentation: any car over three years old must have a current MOT certificate. Any other relevant documents, including registration papers, handbook, repair bills and service history, should be handed on if available
- Mileage: a dealer must try to be certain that the mileage on a car he is selling is correct. With a car that has been traded in he should get a statement from the previous owner to back this up. If the mileage cannot be guaranteed then this must be clearly declared to the potential customer, in addition to placing a warning sticker to this effect next to the odometer reading. If a dealer either deliberately or unwittingly sells a clocked car, he is doing so illegally
- Pre-sale Inspection: a car must have undergone a pre-sale inspection, the inspection report should be prominently displayed and the potential customer given a copy for his retention
- Guarantees: if a printed or written guarantee is provided during the sale of a used car, it is in addition to any legal or statutory rights to which the buyer is entitled and this must be stated.

6.2 Your Basic Legal Rights when Buying from a Dealer

The Sale of Goods Act, revised in 1979, supports three conditions when applied to the sale of used cars:

1) That the car is fit for use (that it at least drives, but will also suit the purpose for which you intend to use it).

2) That the car is of merchantable quality (or that it is of reasonable quality in relation to its price). This is

actually quite subjective when it concerns a used car and is further muddied by the fact that you will be expecting to spend some money on repairs. This part of the law is designed to protect you from buying what looks like a nearly new car on first appearance but which in fact is riddled with mechanical defects.

3) That the dealer's description of the vehicle is accurate and not misleading in any way; for example, if you are informed that the car has a reconditioned engine, new gearbox or new exhaust then you are entitled to proof. Likewise if you buy a car on the understanding that it has a 2.0-litre engine and later discover it to be only 1.6 litres, then you will have grounds for a claim. Sales talk may be persuasive but must still be accurate and truthful – the salesman must not deliberately deceive you.

6.3 Signing Away Your Legal Rights

Whatever a dealer might ask you to sign (usually that you are happy with the vehicle in its present condition), remember that it does not exonerate him from his responsibilities to you where the Sale of Goods Act is concerned. Dealers do know the rules and some of them may rely on your basic unfamiliarity with the trade, and the law in general, to evade this act. Try to make it clear that you understand the act before you sign anything.

Timing a Claim

If you discover that the Sale of Goods Act has been genuinely broken, it is in your interest to make a claim as soon as you discover the problem, since the longer you delay the more difficult it may be to get compensation. You will almost certainly have to prove that the fault was there before you drove the car away. A long delay before claiming could be interpreted as showing that you were quite happy to accept the car in this condition. What you can try to do in the first instance is to get the dealer to list every significant fault in writing, which will help satisfy condition 2 of the Sale of Goods Act. You might then make a claim for a fault that you were not told about, and circumvent any disputes arising from verbal misunderstandings. Some faults are so glaring that you should have been aware of them at the time of the sale; for example, dented bodywork, a worn-out tyre or overheating radiator, and it would be difficult, if not impossible, to claim for these afterwards. Others may be less obvious; for example, a worn steering rack or split drive shaft gaiter or intermittent gearbox fault, and it is these for which you may be entitled to claim. You could *not* claim, though, for faults not revealed during a professional vehicle inspection.

6.4 How to Claim

Even if the car you have bought has a very serious fault it is often not possible to just return the car and demand your money back (although you might be offered this solution if your approach is right!). You will have to argue your case, and the dealer should be prepared to offer you either financial or mechanical help towards putting things right. Do not forget that dissatisfied customers who look as though they mean business are the last thing that a dealer with a hard-earned reputation is going to need.

6.5 How to Claim when the Dealer Refuses to Co-operate

If the dealer decides that the fault is one that you should have identified at the time, but you disagree, then you will first have to determine what the repair will cost. Get an independent report to verify the defect (a professional vehicle inspection might have already done this for you, incidentally), then write the dealer a note to the effect that you have already returned with the car to complain; enclose the report while keeping copies of all correspondence. You may also suggest that if a sensible agreement cannot be reached within a few days you will be taking the matter to court. Any reasonable dealer would – or should – be prepared to concede at least something at this stage, if only to maintain his good name.

As an example, let us suppose that a day or two after buying a car you choose to check the tracking and have the wheels balanced (see chapters 3 and 9). The tyre specialist, if he is honest, tells you that the tracking (an inexpensive item) cannot be done because the steering rack is so seriously worn that your wheels cannot be properly aligned. Explain that you have just bought the car, that you were unaware at the time of the defect and that you plan to return it immediately. Ask him to put the fault in writing – preferably on letterheaded paper – stating the nature of the problem, with an estimate of the likely cost of repair (which at most is only a phone call away). Ask him to sign and date the note and then, when you return to the dealer, hand him the originals and explain that since you do not want to be driving around in a defective and therefore unsafe vehicle you insist upon rectification of the fault within a time limit, say ten days. Give your phone number and ask him to make the necessary arrangements but, whatever you do, *make sure that you deal with the same person each time*, namely, the one who sold you the car. Let him know that if the arrangements are not made within this time, you will be taking the car elsewhere for repair, that is, that fair warning has been given, and that after repair you will be referring the matter to a small claims court.

If you have still not been offered any compensation at this point, and in the event of your actually having to go elsewhere for the repairs, then keep your receipts and go ahead with the courts (or start by asking at the Citizens' Advice Bureau). You will not need a lawyer's representation but you will have to pay a fee of up to £40, and if you lose the case you will only have to pay the other side's travelling and possibly witness expenses. If you win, you will get your costs back on the repairs. Incidentally, the small claims court will deal with claims of up to £1,000 (in England and Wales), which will cover most repair costs on second-hand cars. However, if your engine were to suddenly expire you could be looking at over £1,000 for a good replacement with fitting; and you would need a laywer's representation. In this event you could seek advice from one of the motor trade associations listed above, or if you are a member of the AA you could get free legal advice on how to proceed.

As an alternative to the courts, and once you have argued the appropriate conditions of the Sale of Goods Act, a useful ploy is to suggest that if the matter is not dealt with satisfactorily you will be seeking advice from your local Office of Fair Trading (it would help if you quoted their address, too). You could also threaten to expose the dealer in a local or county paper (name it) and, if you really are getting nowhere, try just that.

6.6 Your Legal Rights when Buying on Credit

If you buy a used car on credit arranged through a dealer (hire purchase or similar), you will be using a finance company and will probably not own the car until the last payment is made. If you experience some trouble getting a dealer to honour his responsibilities to you under the Sale of Goods Act then you will be able to sue the finance company, who would normally be jointly responsible for any conditions of the act that have been broken. The same course of action could be sought through a credit card company if you pay for the car using a personal credit card, for example, Access, American Express, etc., since the credit card company would also be jointly liable for any defects that break the conditions of the act. Your first course of action, after getting no help from the dealer, is to write to the credit card company or finance house directly, explaining as fully as you can the events so far and enclosing photocopies of all relevant documentary evidence. Provided that your claim was for at least £100, and a feasible one, then you should get some help.

6.7 How Good is a Guarantee or Warranty?

This is a tricky area to deal with since the extent of protection offered to you and the premium you pay can vary considerably according to the warranty company used, the level of cover chosen and even the dealer who arranged the cover. What you need to remember about guarantees is that they are *additional* to your basic protection afforded by the Sale of Goods Act, and if you spot the fault early enough you might be better off claiming under these conditions than under the guarantee itself. The small print of a guarantee may actually disguise your benefits instead of making them clearer, and may reveal that it covers only the cost of parts – you have to meet the cost of the labour charges yourself.

Warranties that provide extended cover (mechanical breakdown insurance) are not usually issued by the dealer but are arranged through an insurance company, so in the event of a claim you deal through them instead. When deciding whether to buy a warranty, and often you must decide there and then, look at the small print and ask some pointed questions about any exclusions or provisos in the terms and conditions that might later invalidate your claim for compensation. For example, in cover against corrosion, is it a prerequisite that you have regular inspections carried out, and at your own expense? Also, are service intervals to be carried out at predetermined dates and at a main dealership? What about fair wear and tear, mileage limits or any other, even if seemingly incidental, exclusions that might apply? When choosing an extended warranty, look firstly for one offered by a reputable, long-standing company or one backed by a major motor association such as SMMT; and also talk with colleagues or anyone you know who has had one and ask them about the conditions and benefits and how they have fared.

When buying a second-hand car with some manufacturer's or extended warranty still remaining on it, check with the dealer that all the necessary conditions have been fulfilled by the previous owner(s) – in writing if you can – so that for the price you are paying you are actually receiving something worthwhile.

The RMIF has introduced a minimum standard for the warranties issued by its member garages which would provide for both parts and labour in any claim; and extend cover to periods of three months for a car recording under 20,000 miles, two months for under 40,000 miles and a month for under 60,000. Significant, too, has been the improvement of the pre-inspection guide on used cars and the condition that all chargeable extras be displayed without ambiguity.

6.8 Your Legal Rights when Buying Privately

When you buy a second-hand car from a private individual, your legal redress is very limited and so it is the purpose of this section to help protect the innocent buyer against the less scrupulous (or possibly ignorant) individual by helping you understand just how the law works for you.

The only thing that the seller has to guarantee you is that the sales talk and description of the car are accurate, as in part 3 of the Sale of Goods Act. In effect, there is no guarantee that the car you are looking at is priced fairly, or that it is fit for use, since these things you will have to determine for yourself. And for these reasons a private individual cannot sell you the car for the same price as a dealer would – unless of course you let him. It is a good idea to take someone along with you to act as a witness to anything that is said or promised, and also (where appropriate) you should retain any original newspaper advert in case you need to contest any aspect of its description later. You are able to claim compensation from an individual if you can prove that a specific promise that later turns out to be untrue was made to you about a particular component as long as you complain within a reasonably short space of time. For example, if the seller lies about the mileage, or claims that a reconditioned engine has recently been installed, and you are subsequently able to prove otherwise, then you would have good grounds for a claim. However, supposing you buy a car and the very next day it will not start at all? Well, if no specific promises were made about its reliability then technically the seller has not broken the law and you will have to try to persuade him that, on moral grounds, he ought to pay you some compensation. This is an unlikely possibility but it does occasionally happen.

How to Get Verbal Guarantees

Since you do not have very much protection with a private buy, you will have to safeguard the transaction yourself. So as well as taking someone along with you to act as a second pair of eyes and ears, be sure to note at some stage of your examination or test drive anything that does not feel healthy: a reluctant gear change, suspiciously low mileage figure for the age and condition of the car, rumbling (blowing) exhaust, etc. Make a point of asking the seller about them – he has to answer you even if he thinks this behaviour somewhat pushy. In all probability he will be ignorant of his legal responsibilities and anxious to hurry the sale along, and may agree that the points you question are in fact in good order. This is *not* a trap since you are not asking the man to guarantee every working component of the car – only those (expensive) parts that you feel could be wearing or already defective but that you are still unsure about. You are giving him the chance to declare now any faults over which you might have to claim if need be.

Claim Procedure

If you discover a fairly major fault with any component that you couldn't have known about *at the time* and you figure it is worth trying to get some compensation from the owner, remember that he might just co-operate if you make your approach reasonable but firm. Return with the car as soon as possible, within two or three days at the most. If the seller refuses to listen, claiming that the car is now your problem, you will have to proceed as before: get an independent report to confirm that the fault existed before you bought the car and give written notice of the problem to the seller, following the same procedure as you would if this were a dealer. Merely handing over the letter and explaining your rights under the Sale of Goods Act should be enough to persuade all but the most hardened of individuals to offer you some compensation.

There are two main provisos here – the first is that, especially when buying privately, you must expect to replace some of the components that are subject to regular wear (tyres, exhaust, etc.) and this will apply even more for older and hence cheaper cars. Secondly, taking court action against somebody is not a fun adventure in exercising your legal rights, or an easy way to escape paying for replacements on your new car. You should make sure that your claim is a valid, cost effective one, and that it is worth the effort and potential aggravation involved, bearing in mind that you might not win. Remember too that the AA and Citizens' Advice Bureau can be the best places to begin with legal help and that you should only apply pressure in degrees, as necessary.

6.9 Some Useful Addresses and Telephone Numbers

The Office of Fair Trading
(for local Trading
Standards Authority)
Field House
15–25 Bream's Buildings
London
EC4A 1PR
Tel. 071 242 2858

Retail Motor Industry
Federation (RMIF)
201 Great Portland Street
London
W1N 6AB
Tel. 071 580 9122

Society of Motor
Manufacturers & Traders
(SMMT) (regional)
Forbes House
Halkin Street
London
SW1X 7DS
Tel. 071 235 7000

Scottish Motor Trade
Association (SMTA)
3 Palmerston Place
Edinburgh
EH12 5AQ
Tel. 031 225 3643

Vehicle Builders' &
Repairers' Association
(VBRA)
Belmont House
Guildersome
Leeds
LS27 7TW
Tel. 0532 538333

AA (Head Office)
Fanum House
Basingstoke
RG21 2EA
Tel. 0256 20123

Federation of Engine
Remanufacturers (FER)
Jefferson House
18 Orchard Lane
Guiseley
Leeds
LS20 9HZ
Tel. 0943 870825

Citizens' Advice Bureau
(CAB)
Look in phone book for
local branch.

Small Claims Court
Look in phone book for
nearest one.

7 Dealing with the Dealer (or Private Seller)

As emphasized throughout this book, you must remember that the sale of any used car is a two-way transaction and that you should certainly be under no obligation to buy the first thing you look at. You may be put under considerable pressure to buy, and the salesman will use his charm to persuade you that he is honest. However, your faith in the man's integrity may sell the car.

When buying from dealers seek out places that have shown themselves to be trustworthy and reliable, preferably one that a colleague or friend can recommend to you: good publicity for a garage can be worth several thousands of pounds in expensive advertising. Check out the general standard of their cars and if they give (or need to give) after-sales service. Also determine whether the garage belongs to a trade association, the RMIF, for example. The following are a few tips to bear in mind when negotiating with either a dealer or private seller:

- Whoever you buy from make sure that everything about the car (its condition, history, the seller, the neighbourhood, etc.), all adds up – if anything looks suspect either get to the bottom of it now or walk away from the car: there really are too many good cars to choose from for you to have to tolerate deceit. You should be allowed to examine the car to *your* satisfaction and to study all the documentation relating to the car's history and previous usage

- Don't be fooled by all you see or hear: a windscreen sticker or seller boasting a 'well-maintained' car can mean next to nothing unless backed up by a service history, and might simply relate to the vehicle's external appearance. *Remember: no service history, no inflated windscreen sticker price*
- When buying from a dealer, you should have a very clear idea of the type of car you want, and an equally good idea of how much you are prepared to spend. However, you needn't directly communicate this to the dealer otherwise you could end up driving away in something that was not quite what you wanted, and having parted with more money than you originally intended. Make clear, instead, that you're simply looking for a good deal – then keep quiet
- Learn something about your prospective model since the better you can demonstrate to the seller your knowledge (for example, what level of equipment or accessories you can expect on the Ghia model; whether power steering comes as standard; or if the 1987-model engines onwards were definitely fuel injected), the greater will be your power at negotiating time. Query, too, seemingly minor discrepancies like missing badges from the boot or tailgate, for example, 2.0 GLX or 1.8 DL – does their absence mean that the panel has been hastily resprayed following an accident? And what is a five-speed gear selector lever doing in a car whose gearbox you *know* to have only four speeds?
- It was stated in chapter 2 that around one in four cars is estimated to be clocked, that is, displays a falsely low mileage in an attempt to inflate the dealer's or seller's profit. If the mileage cannot be guaranteed – and the odometer may even show a disclaimer to this effect – then walk away no matter

how 'straight' the rest of the car. With so many genuine cars available for purchase, why take an unneccessary chance on one that isn't?

● The dealer will probably want to sell you a warranty. Ask *exactly* what it covers and how much it will cost (up to 70 per cent of the premium you'll pay could be dealer profit). On a relatively new car (up to three years old) may be the balance of the manufacturer's extended warranty, which could be worth buying as long as you can be absolutely sure that all the terms and conditions attached to it have been satisfied to date. And even in the case of an older vehicle, perhaps your best guarantee of all will come not from a piece of paper but from the thoroughness of the mechanic to whom you will entrust regular servicing and maintenance. In any case, get down *in writing* any additional promises that are made – it could save you much time, aggravation and money later on. Finally, the law is not yet crystal clear concerning cars that are sold subject to outstanding finance agreements. As a general guide, though, if such a car is bought in all innocence you might be allowed to retain it while the finance company reclaims the amount outstanding from the seller; if, however, the car was subject to a *lease* agreement then the car would not have been that individual's to sell in the first instance and it would be well within the rights of the leasing company to repossess the vehicle at the first opportunity. While new legislation to protect the buyer and finance company alike may be just around the corner, your best bet would be to determine *in writing* the position with any loans outstanding. HPI Autodata (see 2.4) should also be able to help

● Sometimes it is agreed that repairs or service work
will be done between the time of sale and the time
the car is collected. Don't make the same mistake as
I once did and simply take the dealer's word for it

■ HOT TIP ■

**Always make sure that you get some form of receipt
for work done, and this should bear the name of the
garage doing the work, with a date, signature and
record of the current mileage in the case of service
work.**

Also, this receipt will form the start of your maintenance records – or service history – which will be
worth money to you when you come to resell the car

● Whether you are negotiating with a dealer or an
individual, always knock down his asking price even
if he doesn't invite offers. The huge majority of
sellers (including dealers) will have raised their prices
beforehand to allow for this
● Make sure that all extras (for example, stereo-cassette
players, rugs, protective mats, roof-racks, alloy
wheels, etc.) that a dealer or seller may offer to
throw in to secure his price are in fact what you
actually need or want – you'll only be getting what
you pay for
● If a dealer knows you're in the market for a specific
model, he may telephone you to come and see the car
currently on his forecourt. It could turn out to be
neither the engine size, specification nor colour you
had stipulated, but of course he now has some extra
time to work on you if you agree to a test drive. Instead,

when he phones, have him tell you the car's particulars *first*

● Read very carefully any small print in an advert
offering an exceptional part-exchange or finance deal,
particularly if it involves your present car – there
could be all manner of conditions attached that mean
you'll end up paying more in the long run; for
example, will that 'mint' 90/G 2.0i 16v Calibra coupé
cost you your 93/K 2.0 Si Mondeo in part-exchange?

● Lastly, always be suspicious of idle boasts that some
sellers seem to think will impress you. A favourite
one is that they have never had to touch the car
between annual service intervals: anyone who tells
you this either drives only twenty miles a year, has a
very short memory or is not telling you the truth.
Such neglect in most cars usually means they will
need a lot of attention sooner rather than later.

8 Trading at Auctions

■■■■ Introduction

Some aspects of trading at auctions are specific to selling, some to buying, and there is a need to understand the general principles involved.

8.1 General

Car auctions are primarily used by motor vehicle wholesalers although many dealers and an increasing number of private buyers and sellers are to be seen at auctions. There are two categories of car auction: major trade centres that are very professionally run, of which ADT at Measham is probably the biggest; and smaller affairs that are often an extension of a local general auctioneer's activities (for example, selling household-furniture-type articles).

■■■■ HOT TIP ■■■■■■■■■■■■■■

It is a sound principle to buy from a major professional auction and to sell at a smaller independent auction.

The reasons are explained in detail later in this chapter. Before attempting to buy or sell a used car at an auction it is important to know the main rules that apply.

The fall of the auctioneer's hammer constitutes a legal and binding contract between the last person to bid and the seller. Neither of them can change their mind and both have the support of law to enforce completion of the sale. To protect both buyer and seller the conditions of sale are prominently displayed in the auction hall.

8.2 Guarantees

In respect of motor vehicles there are two main forms of description that the auctioneer will use. 'Sold as seen (and without warranty)', which means exactly what it says. Whatever is wrong with the vehicle, any bidder is purchasing the faults as part of the price they pay for the car. In this way the seller is offering the car as it can be seen, together with any and all faults it may have that cannot be seen, as a single item. There is no responsibility on the seller's part to offer a safe, legally roadworthy or even complete car.

The second description is 'sold all good'. This description will probably only apply to cars of around five years old or less and only if the auctioneer announces it immediately prior to asking for bids. Without such an announcement the 'sold as seen' rule applies. 'Sold all good' excludes all parts of the car that are visible: bodywork, rust, tyres, exhaust and most service items except major mechanical components. 'All good', then, refers to the engine, gearbox, axle and sometimes steering and suspension, and even then, in the event of a complaint, the resident engineer who arbitrates would be making due allowance for the age and mileage of the car.

8.3 Buying at Auctions

A large professional car auction (or indeed any belonging to the Society of Motor Auctions) will be the safest place to buy. They sell many hundreds (and often several thousands) of cars every sales day (usually two or three times a week). The auctioneers don't have time to mess about or try to push the bidding up. They are professionals dealing with professionals and prices are much lower than at smaller auctions. The selection of cars for sale is vast and whatever car you are looking for there will probably be several of the model and year you want.

Try to decide what you want *before* you go. Look at, and even test-drive, more than one model at your local used-car dealer. Price the car you want. At a major auction you should expect to pay between 50–75 per cent of the dealer's forecourt price. It is a good idea to have a second choice that you have also researched and priced. This will allow you the freedom to bid for a bargain if one comes along. Take enough cash to cover 10 per cent of the amount you are prepared to spend or £500, whichever is the greater. The auctioneer will require this as soon as you have successfully bid on a car. The balance may be paid by cheque but you will not be allowed to take the car away until your cheque has cleared. This will give you time to arrange the insurance and, if necessary, the road fund licence (road tax). You will have to pay an indemnity insurance of up to about £25, which will insure you against there being any outstanding HP on the car, it having been an insurance total loss, clocked or stolen. Well worth it!

Don't rush to bid for the first car that looks like a bargain. Many cars are sold without reserve (they are here to be sold for the highest bid) and there are usually plenty of bargains.

■■■ HOT TIP ■■■

Give yourself time to adjust to the lower prices and the confusion you may be feeling. As each car that fits your needs enters the ring and bidding starts, set a mental price limit that you are prepared to pay – *at least* **40 per cent below dealer forecourt price – and wait. If the bidding goes above the price you set, DO NOT BID. If the bidding stops below the price you set – then is the time to bid. STOP ONE BID BEFORE YOUR SET PRICE. If you become involved in bidding against someone else, there is a danger that you'll start thinking of the car as yours and keep bidding beyond your price range to protect your property.**

Further Buying Hints

Remember, you're here to buy a car that will give plenty of service, and for less money than you'd pay a dealer or privately. The following tips are included to help prevent a bad choice:

Study For Detail and Incongruencies

Examine closely for missing headrests, stereos, roof-rack attachments, floor mats, badges, mudflaps and even auxiliary driving lights – it is not uncommon for cars entered at auction to have been grave-robbed by the previous owner(s).

Beware inconsistencies. I recently saw an 81X-reg MK II Ford Granada sporting a Ghia S badge (which belonged to the 1970s model styling) and a post-1983 grille; both items betrayed by the very definitely 1970s interior and chrome rear light cluster styling. Remember, *know your car* and be prepared to walk away if the example isn't 'clean'.

At another independent southern auction I encountered a similar MK II Granada, this time a 2.8i Ghia boasting a genuine 39,000 miles, full leather interior, almost immaculate bodywork and entered by a franchised Ford dealership. Closer inspection, however, revealed both odometer and leather upholstery to be well past the recorded 39,000 miles. The *real* question to be asking here is why a main dealer – who should have little trouble offloading a car of this calibre – should prefer to use the auctions for much less profit? Or, to put it another way, why did he not want to risk selling from his own forecourt? Somewhere therein lies the answer!

Mileage Giveaways

Look for clusters of clues that will reveal not only the true mileage of the car but also the manner in which it has been earned; for example, towbar attachments, GB nationality stickers and also caravan club affiliation stickers, which I once saw on one 98,000-miler in otherwise good overall condition. The heavy blue exhaust smoke upon start-up helped confirm that this car would not have been worth buying at any price.

Leaking Engines

It is possible to see cars driven into auction on the day of entry. Study the ground underneath the engine as it cools down – are there puddles of oil, water, power steering or transmission fluid developing? If so, you might expect some big bills (and clues, perhaps, as to the reason the car is being entered).

Missing Logbooks

As we saw in 2.4, the logbook or V5 registration certificate is the key to a car's pedigree and, therefore, its saleability. A missing logbook, or one that needs to be applied for, *could* be disguising one or more of the following:

● Many former owners (*not* a selling-point)
● A finance company repossession (see chapter 7)
● An insurance write-off, stolen, or imported and hence older or lower specification car
● Any other details the previous owner doesn't want disclosed – perhaps even being altered while you bid!

Engineer's Report

Finally, do make use of any engineer's test report that a seller might have gone to the trouble to get. Such reports (displayed on the windscreen) usually cover the engine, transmission, steering, brakes, electrics, bodywork and tyre condition. One such report on a luxury hatchback I saw recently declared both engine and gearbox to be 'needing some attention'; this lack of specificity indicated to me that more than just a regular service would be needed on this car. Bearing in mind that the engine and gearbox are probably the two most expensive items to repair, either build into your bid price a margin for potential remedy or read the writing on the wall and walk away.

Vans and Light Commercial Vehicles

While much the same buying procedures will apply equally to vans and other light commercial vehicles, note in addition that most will be:

- subject to a VAT surcharge
- mainly diesels and/or turbo-diesels
- subjected to harder mileages, greater wear and tear and, perhaps, driver abuse (overloading and subsequent tolls on the powertrain, axle and suspension being the most common).

Do attend the larger, better-established sites such as ADT, which regularly hold several categories of sale; for example, ex-BT Escort/Maestro lines, Top Van sales and manufacturers' credit/contract hire lines. You can also pick up a list of the running order of the vehicles that will help you keep records of which vans are fetching which prices. A current copy of *What Van?* might help, too.

What to look for:

- Warranted mileage (this is a must)
- Full service history and (if over three years old) a long MOT – both will help confirm the true mileage
- As few owners/drivers as possible
- Vans brought in direct from large established companies such as Royal Mail, BT, Mercury, borough council fleets. There will be less chance of clocking, neglect, etc., and entries might simply reflect the company's policy to replace a vehicle after three or so years
- State of the payload and driver cabin areas – both can help prove condition and real mileage
- Balance of warranty from either manufacturer or lease/contract hire firm
- Vans that will best match your requirements. There could be a world of difference in the loading capacity, handling, visibility and even reliability of a Nissan Sunny or Bedford Astramax compared to a Ford Escort. Test-drive different models before you buy.

What to avoid:

- Finance company repossessions: it means no service history, mileage guarantee or balance of warranty
- Very low mileage: unless the vehicle itself is but months old, otherwise this could mean much stop-start city mileage and resultant unhealthy engine
- Extra towbar/roof-rack attachments: evidence of harder mileage and wear and tear on engine, transmission, axle, suspension and brakes
- Turbo-diesels: fine when new and performance is lively. Good maintenance is the key: however, there is much potential for abuse and subsequent (enormous) repair costs. Besides, if your mileage really is limited to city driving, is this a facility you actually need?
- Recent vans (up to four years old) which have needed either an engine modification or rebuild.

8.4 Sources

Where do all the cars come from and why are they so cheap? Dealers who are overstocked and need to turn stock into cash is one answer. They will often sell their better stock at auction and rely on their salesmen to sell the rest. Others come from car hire companies, banks, finance houses, bailiffs, official receivers or in fact anyone who needs to turn an unwanted asset into cash quickly, cleanly and with as little effort as possible. Many of these sellers will stipulate 'sold as seen' to avoid the risk of a time-consuming complaint. This does not necessarily mean there is anything wrong with the vehicle, it means that they don't care whether there is or not – they just want to be rid of it. Many cars offered are only a few weeks old (with correspondingly low mileages) and are 'sold as seen' for this reason.

Generally it is the younger, lower-mileage cars brought in *direct* from the company or private individual that will be a safer buy than those having passed through the hands of the motor trade first (in which all manner of things *could* have happened since).

Good examples also include: three- to five-year-old company and fleet cars with service histories (even if the mileage is high); ex-management or executive models entered in a Union Jack sale (under two years and 20,000 warranted miles); and those entered by car-hire firms such as Avis, Hertz, Dollar, etc., which ought to be arriving with very limited warranted mileages and complete service histories (although the opportunities for mechanical abuse are somewhat multiplied by the sheer numbers of different drivers who, with their varying degrees of driving skill and concern for the car, will have taken to the wheel).

Finally, even those cars that have been repossessed by bailiffs and finance companies, in which maybe little more than a single service interval had been skipped, could still represent good value.

8.5 Private Treaty (Provisional) Sales

Quite often a car will, for whatever reason, fail to reach its reserve (or minimum) price set by the seller. At such times the auctioneer will try to contact the seller to negotiate a final price acceptable to both parties. If this happens, remember that you're in a stronger position than the seller, who may have no choice other than to go lower if to avoid a further entry fee or the inconvenience of re-advertising the unsold car. Prepare to haggle, using any defect, however minor, as a starting-point for bringing the price down.

Although auctions are risky in many ways, there are huge savings to be made. You do need some courage to buy at auction but the rewards can be well worth the effort. An auction can even make for an entertaining day out!

8.6 Selling

The bigger the auction site the lower the prices. Smaller, independent auctions have fewer cars to offer, more private buyers attend and the auctioneer works harder at obtaining the best price for the seller. The former is on a commission (typically 6–8 per cent of the car's selling price).

There are two main reasons for selling at auction. It's quick and easy – or there is something wrong with your car that would not merit your selling it privately. If you are selling at auction because it's easy (and in fact you don't even have to attend) then clean, polish and valet your car first – a bright, tidy-looking car will sell for more than a dirty one (see chapter 10).

If you are selling because there is something mechanically wrong with your car, clean and polish it anyway if the bodywork is good. If the bodywork is damaged, scratched or rusted then a modest layer of road grime may help to hide it.

However, because of the lack of guarantees that a seller is able to provide, cars sold at auction will not fetch their best price.

Telephone the auction site and ask when you should bring the car in; they may want it the day before the sale. And when you take the car ensure you bring the

registration papers, current and past MOT certificates
and any service or maintenance records you may have.
You will be asked to fill in a simple entry form (see
figure 20), pay an entrance fee (between £15–£25) and
to sign an acceptance of the conditions of sale. If you
wish to place a reserve (or minimum) price, then normally you may do so. The auctioneer/receptionist will
not normally accept an over-optimistic reserve, though.
If your car is very old (up to fifteen years, or so) it often
helps the sale not to set a reserve. The auctioneer may
start the bidding at a silly price such as £30 and wait
for bidding to come from all corners. It is a bit risky
but if the car is worth very little anyway this may be
better than your losing the entry fee and having to drive
the car home again!

Figure 20 *Auction lot ticket showing typical vehicular details*

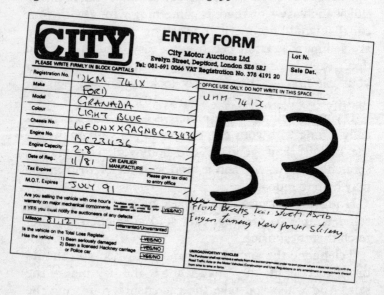

9 The Nine Things You Should Do Immediately on Buying a Used Car (If You Want to Save a Lot of Money)

Introduction

Now that you have the keys in your hand, what are the most important things to see to next? There are nine of them and they are as follows:

9.1 Documentation

Notify your insurance company of the new vehicle particulars. You will need to tell them the make, model and trim level (for example, L, GL, GLX), engine size, colour, year of registration, full registration number, present value of the vehicle (usually the market value or what you paid for it) and the type of insurance cover you want; for example, third party only, fully comprehensive, etc. You should submit all this information to them *prior* to driving the car. The dealer may have provided cover for your test drive but it is your responsibility now and, besides, driving a car without insurance is illegal.

■ HOT TIP ■

If an uninsured car is involved in a collision, you will have no right to claim for damage to your car and you may have to pay for all damage to other cars, persons or property.

The law applies also to tax discs and you can be fined for not displaying one even if, for instance, the disc has peeled away from the window.

The other document you must complete and return as quickly as possible is the vehicle registration paper (or V5), which will later show you to be the new owner of the car. Fill in the reverse side (name, address and date you bought or acquired the vehicle) and tick the box to signify that you are the new keeper. Then post to the following address: DVLC, Swansea SA99 1AR. It is actually an offence not to inform the DVLC of your new ownership or even of a change of address. It is the DVLC who remind you of road tax renewal, for instance.

9.2 Wheel Alignment and Balancing

It is a good idea to have your car checked for proper wheel alignment (tracking) and balancing – the importance of this has already been established in chapter 3.

When having the tracking seen to, ask about the state of your car's track rod ends since, if they are worn, realigning the wheels will be ineffective. Have the rear wheels balanced as well as the front ones since, although not quite so critical, this will help minimize unnecessary vibrations and shudders through the bodywork as a whole. Tracking and wheel balancing carried out at a good tyre-fitting bay should cost between £20–£35, depending on the work carried out.

9.3 Underbody Rust Prevention and Cheaper Driving)

When you get home, jack the car up and, with a hard water jet, hose off all the dirt and grime from underneath the car body – you might be surprised at just how much has accumulated. Attend in particular to mud that has hardened at the wheel arches, under bumpers and in other inaccessible areas. You will slow down the corrosion that attacks from underneath – wet mud, which contains salt, sticks to the underbody and becomes trapped thereby accelerating corrosion from the outside in. Many owners repeat this procedure in the late autumn prior to the worst onslaught of winter corrosion. If you do not have the tools, time or ability to do this yourself, then bear in mind that some garages offer a fairly low-cost chassis steam-cleaning service.

And if not already fitted, then buying a pair of front mudguards will do much to prevent mud, slush and stones from being thrown up against the underbody and will reduce long-term corrosion. Prices generally start at around £15–£20 a pair.

9.4 Defective Parts

If you have just bought a car in the knowledge that certain parts need renewing then see to these now. This will be essential for tyres, brakes, lights, steering racks, clutches, cooling systems and suspension components. Tough new MOT regulations now make replacement mandatory for items such as broken wing mirrors, headlight lenses and indicators, blown bulbs and even damaged bumper trim: several of these items – if defective – render the car not only unroadworthy and therefore dangerous to drive, but also illegal.

◼◼◼ HOT TIP ◼◼◼

If your car is more than a few years old, don't rule out the possibility of sourcing replacement parts from a breaker or scrapyard. Many items, from fog-lamps to alternators to door panels or complete engines, can be bought in good order and at hugely discounted prices, often with a guarantee. The parts – which themselves may be even younger than your car – would have come from all types of vehicle scrapped for any number of reasons and not necessarily because of failure of the component you're seeking. Many breakers offer a convenient off-the-shelf service.

9.5 Servicing

Even if you have an invoice to prove that the car has had a recent service, it is still worth checking over some of the essentials. Spark-plugs, air and oil filters are easy enough to check and cheap to replace. A full service done now is a good opportunity to fix those minor things like perishing radiator hoses, fraying fan belts and blown interior light-bulbs, as well as a major item such as a new cam belt. It is also a good opportunity to make sure that nothing serious was overlooked during your initial assessment – a defective water pump, for example, brittle fuel pipes or low brake fluid level.

Remember to tell the garage at the outset that you'll

require a receipt that will list clearly all the parts and labour prices for which you will be charged.

9.6 Engine Tune-up

It is advisable to book an appointment to have your engine tuned. Go to somebody who specializes in engine tuning exclusively, and if you can choose a firm by referral then all the better. There are many to choose from in the *Yellow Pages*, but beware of garages charging too *little* rather than too much for a tune-up. Depending on your model you should be paying around £35–£45, exclusive of parts and VAT.

The value of a thorough tune-up is that the car will give you a better mpg (or at least a figure well approaching the manufacturer's). It will also cure misfiring, improve starting characteristics and enhance performance and reliability: in short, your engine should be operating at its peak.

Among the items a tune-up will have checked – and some firms claim this can be as many as eighty – include: cylinder compression ratios (each one's performance relayed to a computer printout); starter motor; battery condition and voltage; alternator (or dynamo) output; ignition items (spark-plug efficiency, HT leads, coil, distributor and rotor-arm condition); breather system, manifolds, flat spots; evidence of torn or blown gaskets; carburettor settings and air/fuel mixtures for different engine speeds.

9.7 Engine Steam Clean and Valeting

While the engine tune-up will have revealed most faults and trouble spots, it might also be a good idea to have the engine steam cleaned in order to highlight any tiny insidious leaks. Pinpointing these early on will give you time to repair them before the problem deteriorates. Leaks can occur anywhere, although commonly at the fuel pump, rocker (cam) cover gasket or front timing cover, while others, such as those originating from the rear main bearing/crankshaft seal, can be prohibitively expensive to cure (requiring removal of the engine itself) and might be more cheaply remedied by frequent top-ups with the cheapest quality motor oil instead. Steam cleaning may cost about £15 and may take only twenty minutes with usually no appointment necessary. It is worth noting that you can have both engine and under-side treated at the same time for as little as £25.

Many will choose to have their cars professionally valeted only at the time of selling – however, why not consider a full valet on your 'new' car now? For anywhere between £50 and £100 even an older car will benefit enormously from a steam clean, wash, wax and polishing programme that will remove much of the ingrained and deep-seated dirt, stains and odours accumulated during previous ownership. Psychologically, too, you benefit from enhanced driving pleasure and comfort.

9.8 Securing Your Car or Van

Despite the fact that a car is stolen almost every minute of the day, there are several steps you can take to reduce the likelihood of your own vehicle undergoing an outright theft or break-in. The following list is neither exhaustive nor definitive, but is included to offer some guidance on what is becoming an increasingly sophisticated market place.

Commonsense Methods

At its simplest level, you should ensure each time you leave your car, be it only for a few minutes, that you remove all unnecessary items from display (even a few loose coins or a newspaper left on the seat may be sufficient to prompt a break-in); close all windows and sun-roof, lock all doors (including the boot) and pocket your ignition keys. If leaving your car for several hours, and especially if this means you'll be making your return after dark, try to park in the vicinity of a street lamp – it'll make the potential thief's decision to break in that much harder.

Visual Deterrents

Investing in one of the more visible Krook-lok or Stop-lok type devices, or in fact any other highly visible deterrent such as a heavy-duty chain wrapped tightly around the steering-wheel and gear lever or brake pedal, will do much to ward off some of the more casual attempts to break in. A quality Krook-lok can be purchased for under £30.

Wheel Clamps

You can buy your own wheel clamp, which is both simple to fit and highly effective and can be bought for upwards of £55.

Security Window Etching

A very discreet and highly effective yet inexpensive defence is to have your windows, windscreens and both front and rear headlight assemblies professionally etched with your vehicle registration or engine number. This will cost about £10. Its value as a deterrent lies with the considerable inconvenience and expense to which the thief would be put in either having to erase the coding itself (which would arouse suspicion in the next interested buyer), or indeed in having to replace each of the items marked. So popular is this method, it is likely your next car will already be etched in this way.

Alarms

The bad publicity surrounding some car alarms and their irresponsible owners may be deserved, leaving their effectiveness somewhat open to question. Overall, though, they probably do help prevent theft and in fact many insurers now offer premium discounts provided a specified alarm is fitted. If in doubt, obtain and have fitted one approved to a British Standard rather than buying one of the cheaper DIY efforts whose design and installation may be such that it invalidates a manufacturer's warranty or insurance claim.

Deadlocks

Having deadlocks fitted to the doors ought to give at least some peace of mind since, even if a window becomes smashed, the thief will still be unable to open the doors in order to access the stereo or drive the car away.

Wheel Locking Nuts

Wheel locking nuts are a must where a particularly expensive set of alloy wheels and high-performance tyres (up to £300 each) are to be spared the risk of theft. Remember to take the locking nut key with you when you leave the car parked.

Tracker

Tracker is one of the latest, most powerful techniques to combat car theft and takes its origins from the

American Lo-jack system devised in the last few years. In the event of your car being stolen, the electronic signal implanted in the car can be traced by a police tracking network such that recovery can be achieved within a very short space of time – even minutes. Although Tracker is as yet too recent to be properly evaluated in this country, and while it won't actually *prevent* your car from being broken into or stolen, the fairly high-profile advertising of the system, in addition to the 90 per cent plus claimed recovery rate overseas, suggests that Tracker is likely to be one of *the* effective future anti-theft devices within the reach of most of us. Available as an aftermarket item, there is the probability that many insurance companies will be prepared to offer premium discounts on vehicles to which it is fitted.

9.9 Improving Your Fuel Consumption – How to Save Big Money

As we saw in chapter 1, engine capacity alone only partly determines mpg and, therefore, your overall fuel bill. Indeed, an off-tune, poorly maintained and carelessly driven 1.6-litre engined car can be using more fuel than a well-tuned, mechanically sound and considerately driven 2.0-litre model in the same range.

Real fuel economy has to do with many things, then: good routine maintenance; driving with restraint and forethought; planning your journeys economically; and better observation at the filling station. Observing the following tips will help you improve your mpg – whatever car you drive.

Planning

Careful planning of your trips will eliminate the need for much zipping back and forth and, therefore, using greater quantities of fuel to cover the same ground. Most engines will benefit from a ten- to fifteen-mile warm-up so, if frequent stops are necessary, begin by driving to your furthermost destination first: subsequent stops will waste less fuel upon restarting.

Quickest Route

Main A-roads might provide the most direct routes, but frequently entail much stop-start progress. Try to use less cluttered routes such as B-roads or perhaps motorways, even if they make the journey time or distance slightly longer. You'll be on the move more of the time *and* achieving more mpg since your engine will be warming up more quickly. Remember that rush hour travel, particularly from cold, will seriously dent your mpg figures by increasing mechanical wear and tear in the time it takes the engine to properly warm up.

Light Loads

While it is a good idea to carry some spares and tools (such as fan belts, hoses and spanners) in case of road-side emergency, think for a moment about the loads you *don't* need: yesterday's packed suitcase you forgot to remove; pairs of boots or blankets you need for only occasional use; complete tool-boxes and even portable oil and petrol cans all go towards increasing the weight the engine must overcome – which it does by using extra fuel. When carrying heavy items is unavoidable, pack them so the greatest weight is concentrated towards the middle of the car. It'll provide better stability and also means less wear and tear on the rear suspension.

Of course, leaving on that seldom-used roof-rack not only negates any aerodynamic advantage your car may have, but will contribute to up to 4–5 per cent wastage from the fuel tank. Driving at high speeds with the windows or sun-roof open can result in similar losses.

On the Move

Except in freezing winter conditions, when the oil in the sump might need extra time to thin out and circulate, you will achieve better fuel consumption if you drive off as quickly as possible after starting up. At the end of your journey you will make for equally good economy if you park the car so that it is ready to be driven away in a *forward* direction. Having to reverse and/or perform other, low-speed or tricky manoeuvres from cold will require the use of substantially more fuel.

Electrical Accessories

Switch off all electrical in-car accessories *before* you start the engine, and this applies equally to both cold *and* warm starts. Any accessory, from headlights, heated windscreen, air-conditioning, windscreen wipers or even the radio, will be draining extra current from the battery, which will need a greater charging period from the alternator (or dynamo) system, which in turn will find the necessary energy at the expense of the engine using more fuel. Make sure the engine is running before you switch anything else on.

Steady Speed

Your engine, depending on its size, will be most efficient when running at between 30–50 mph, that is, will give the best return in mpg. Driving at over 70 mph will cause the engine to use a disproportionate amount of fuel, as will a hurried acceleration from standstill. The carburettor can only deal with so much fuel at any given time and so any extra to requirement – provided by a heavy foot on the accelerator pedal – will remain unburned and lost for ever. This is why every competition at the traffic-lights with a budding Nigel Mansell may win you the short-term race, but will cost you more in frequent refuelling at the pumps.

Brakes

After each time you apply the brakes, the engine must work that much harder at moving the car again from rest and, of course, it does this by burning more fuel. Looking as far ahead as possible for potential changes in road conditions may eliminate the need for heavy braking altogether. Particularly at traffic-lights and roundabouts, aim to keep moving, albeit slowing to a crawl if necessary, before having to actually stop. You will use less fuel to re-accelerate than if you had come to a complete rest.

Automatic Gearboxes

At a junction where a stop is unavoidable, such as at a traffic-light, selecting N or neutral will help cut down on fuel wastage and, in addition, help prolong the life of your car's transmission system.

Manual Gearbox

With a manual gearbox there is even greater potential to use fuel more economically than with an automatic, but this will also depend upon your driving skill. Only low speeds warrant the use of low gears. Try to pull away from rest in second gear and then move up into the highest possible ratio for any given speed (though without forcing the engine to labour).

At the Filling Station

Know Your Petrol

Whether you use leaded or unleaded petrol, or diesel fuel, there is probably a particular brand that best suits your engine, helping you squeeze an extra few miles from every tankful. The cheapest may not always be the best, however, so experiment with your car's performance over varying conditions (country lanes, high streets, motorways, wet and dry roads, etc.) then make a note to use only those filling stations offering the best mileage return.

Discount Fuel

Some supermarket retailing chains, such as Sainsbury and Tesco, offer greatly discounted fuel prices on which you might save about £1 on a typical fill-up of eleven gallons, roughly equal to £5–£10 a month. That's £100 a year, or £1,000 a decade.

Optimum Fill-up

The best time to fill up with fuel is when the engine is already warm since frequent cold starts and low-speed manoeuvres consume more fuel and contribute greater engine wear. Favour post-motorway fill-ups then, to those first thing in the morning.

Never fill the fuel tank to capacity – it might result in an overspill, which is simply money down the drain. Fill to just over three quarters full, then straighten the pump hose to drain every last drop – you'll have paid for it. Don't stop there either: why not get the benefit of the 20p or so worth left in the petrol pump bend by the previous user before you activate the pump gun.

Mechanical Condition

Lastly, remember that optimum fuel efficiency can only really be achieved if your car is in sound mechanical condition. Begin by checking the tyre pressures twice weekly (look them up in your handbook or ask at a tyre-fitting bay if you don't know what they should be and then keep to those pressures when carrying normal loads). Even a few pounds over or under the recommended on one or more tyres will accelerate tyre wear, increase fuel consumption and could lead to premature steering and suspension wear (see chapter 3).

Binding (over-adjusted or seized) brakes, holed exhausts, worn shock absorbers or tyres and even low engine oil and coolant levels will all take a toll on the fuel gauge reading.

Although frequent servicing is costly in the short term, it ought to pay for itself in the long run. Put another way, there is simply no financial gain in prolonging the life of spent components, particularly if they are cheap to replace, such as spark-plugs, ignition leads, clogged air and oil filters and filthy, inefficient oil. Even the more expensive items, such as distributors, ignition coils, starter motors and blowing exhaust sections, will have to be replaced anyway, so why not sooner rather than later?

Friction Reducers

It is estimated that some 75 per cent of engine wear occurs in the first few seconds of engine start-up, that is, in the time it takes the oil in the sump to circulate to protect the moving parts. Using a good-quality friction-reducing agent such as Slick 50 at your next oil change will help minimize abrasion by coating the contacting metal surfaces with tough polymer. As a side benefit, around a 2-mpg saving can be expected – even in higher-mileage engines.

High-mileage Driving
Consider your driving patterns as a whole. *Where* are the bulk of your miles chalked up? If your annual mileage is nearer the 20,000 than the 10,000 mark, and you cover a fair proportion of that on motorways, then you might consider buying a diesel version of the model you drive. The more robust, frugal and low-depreciating properties we looked at in chapter 1 should mean that a well-maintained diesel will give you a better return when you come to resell.

For a truly superb treatment of the subject of driving for economy, which goes well beyond the scope of this book, the reader is referred to Sikorsky and Rowlands' *How to Get More Miles Per Gallon* (Arrow, 1980).

10 How to Sell Your Existing Car

Introduction

Having bought your 'new' car, you will probably be keen to sell your existing one as soon as possible. After all, it is likely that the money could be spent profitably on the new one.

10.1 The Best Times to Sell

The best times to sell are usually between April and July. Spring and summer should fetch your car a higher price, but you will be in competition with everyone else, particularly with the dealers who, during August, will be doing their best to dispose of the glut of trade-ins following the seasonal rush of new-car sales.

Other factors that may influence the best times to sell might include fashion, demand and asking price. Even the political situation may have an effect – fears of massive petrol price rises following the Iraqi-precipitated Gulf crisis helped considerably reduce the sales of larger-engined cars returning low mpg.

10.2 Methods of Selling

Here is the range of options open to you when selling:

Part-exchange with a Dealer

means getting rid of the old one in a simple, straight-forward step. You are free from the difficulties of advertising – for what can be up to several weeks – and can drive away immediately with an upgraded model. This method is advantageous if you have an expensive car to offload or if your car is unsound, mechanically or structurally, and will be too expensive for you to repair. The drawback is that you most certainly will receive less money than if your were to sell privately. If you do decide to part-exchange with a dealer, visit two or three before you do since it is not solely the price a dealer will give you for your current model, but the change-over price – how much you are actually paying for the new one when you have deducted the price the dealer discounts for you – that determines the real value of the trade-in. Read the price guides to get a realistic idea of what your car is worth and be prepared to negotiate closer to the trade values rather than holding out for an unreasonably high trade-in. If a dealer seems to be offering you too little, you can always move on – there are plenty of other equally suitable cars available on other dealers' forecourts. Bear in mind also that dealers often take in 'bad' cars in part-exchange since they figure that a buyer's car must have at least *some* value, and also because they may simply need to if it will help secure a sale.

◼◼ HOT TIP ◼◼

Do beware of high part-exchange offers, they are often a ruse to attract you to a car they can't sell. Try to establish a value for your car without specifying which car you wish to purchase.

Selling to a Dealer

Another method is to sell to a dealer even if you are not buying anything. Not all dealers will do this of course and, even if you have a popular model, your chances of getting the very best return are low. Many cars that dealers take in are below the standard that they can sell for a profit, and they turn up on the forecourts of other dealers, backstreet traders or at auction. If your car looks in good condition but the mechanical faults are too expensive for you to correct prior to selling privately, then trading to a dealer who has more resources than you, and perhaps less knowledge of the faults in your car, could be a more attractive proposition.

Part-exchanging Privately

Another method – while admittedly not very common – is to part-exchange or swap your car for another person's. This can save on the inconvenience of buying and selling but is an altogether more risky way to trade since your legal redress in the event of the worst happening is very limited.

Selling at Auctions

This has already been discussed in chapter 8 but, to recap briefly, this is a way of passing on your old car with the minimum of negotiation and inconvenience. Cars sold at auctions do not fetch anywhere near their top price since there are very few worthwhile guarantees on them or, indeed, opportunities for proper inspection. You would probably sell this way if your car was in poor mechanical condition; or you did not have much time for preparing it; or much concern for the price you'll get. Even so, it is worth remembering that you're likely to get a better price here than if you were to trade-in or sell to a dealer.

Selling for Scrap

If your car has been involved in a serious collision, or is fraught with physical and mechanical defects and its present condition means that even dealers will not be able to offer you anything, you may have to consider selling for scrap. This really is a last resort since, depending on the age and popularity of the car and the extent of damage, you might expect to receive only between £15–£50; newer cars (up to five years old) may only fetch £200–£500. Bear in mind the specialized breakers such as those dealing only in certain makes, for instance Ford or Vauxhall, since they may be able to offer you more for the car as a source of spares. Remember, too, that included in the pages of *Auto Trader* and *Exchange & Mart* are sections in which you can specifically advertise crash-damaged vehicles.

Selling via Car Agencies

One of the fastest growing areas in car selling has been that of the specialist agency who, for a fee of up to £50 usually, will offer to advertise your car in both the national and motor press and leave prospective customers to contact you direct. The agency, who most probably spotted your original advert in an existing publication, may claim an already considerable interest in your model of car, virtually guaranteeing its sale there and then – claims that can prove less than substantial even several weeks after their attempted handling of the sale. Further, you may even be offered free holidays or full refunds if there is no sale within a set time limit. Better to advertise the car locally yourself for what should prove a much greater response and for a more affordable outlay. In fact, to avoid contact with this kind of agency, remember to state clearly 'No Canvassers' at the end of your advert.

Selling Privately

This is usually the most profitable way of disposing of your old car and the one that warrants the most discussion. In the following pages, we will be looking at what you will need to know about preparing your car and also the materials you will need; how to write an effective advertisement to increase your chances of selling at the right price and first time; and *how* to sell to a prospective buyer. You will be guided through all the necessary paperwork and shown the legal responsibilities that bind you.

10.3 Pricing Your Car

As part of the preparations for selling your car, and even before you think about advertising, you must realistically consider what the car is worth. Remember you are selling the economical life left in the car, which could be months or years and will depend on its age and how well it has been looked after. If you have not bought a used car in a long time you will probably be out of touch with prices, so one of the first things will be to check out the going rates for cars of a similar age, condition and supply. Get hold of a good price guide (see 2.6) and if your model is more recent than July 1985 there is a good chance it will be represented (if you car is older, you will have to use local newspapers and your own judgement). When you find your model you will have to determine its condition. Between good and fair is a realistic guide to pricing. You should always consider the mileage your car has travelled and this can work in your favour. For instance if you are selling a 1984 model and you have done an average mileage of 10,000 per year, your odometer will display between 80,000–90,000 miles, corresponding to the eight or nine years that have elapsed since the car was first registered. If the car has travelled considerably less, this can be a good selling-point, although, as we have seen, mileage is not an exact measure of an engine's condition. If at some stage you have had a reconditioned engine fitted it will be necessary to consider only the mileage recorded on the new one.

It can be very difficult to judge a car's true worth in the market-place since owners often tend to be less than objective about their cars. It is easy to allow your judgement to be clouded by the sentimental value of the car. My advice is that you estimate on the conservative side. As a rule of thumb, A1 or First Class condition will be reflected by the best price you could expect for a used car: no bodywork blemishes or visible rust, very clean, well-maintained interior, shining paintwork, good tyres and generally low mileage. No private seller will want to make any substantial guarantees (see 6.8) on a car, and so even if the one you are selling really is in immaculate condition, still try not to go overboard with your advertising; let the buyer be impressed by what he sees instead. It will just as easily help secure your asking price.

Cars much older than about 1984 will fetch a good price only if they are in truly excellent condition with full service history, handsome-looking coachwork and interior and a long MOT. If your car has rarity value, for example, a Morris Minor Traveller or BMW CSL coupé, try asking some dealers what they will give you for it and others how much they would charge to obtain one for you. Pricing at somewhere between the two would be most sensible. Classic car magazines could prove an additional first help.

Other Guides

Scan the local newspapers and some of the nationwide publications, such as *Auto Trader* or *Exchange & Mart*, to get a better idea of what other people are asking for similar models and then scan their adverts carefully. The next stage in selling your car will be to spot a good advert (for a similar car) and try to improve on it.

10.4 How to Write the Best Advertisement to Sell Your Car

You can easily pay up to £25 to place an advert in a newspaper or magazine and so it is in your interest to write a good one that will sell your car first time. The purpose of this chapter is to show you how to write a truthful and appealing advert that will compel any seriously interested party to come and view the car.

Where to Advertise

Of all the choices, let us first consider the ones that are either cheap or free. There are some free newspapers that cover all of London and the Home Counties (for example *Loot*) but since they cover such a large area this may effectively limit the response from your locality. However, you have nothing to lose since an advert of up to (about) fifty words is free.

To advertise in a shop, you will pay about 25p per postcard per week and you are limited only by the number of words you can fit on the card. With this type of advert it is often a good ploy to provide a photo of your car to give a better idea of what is being sold. As far as it is possible you want to attract only a few genuinely interested customers rather than several casual inquiries. Some motor factors or motor spares outlets may let you place an advert in their window free of charge. Be sure to draw a brightly coloured border around the card's edge to ensure the advert gets noticed.

Display a FOR SALE sign on brightly coloured paper in the rear windscreen of the car itself, and park the car in a prominent place outside your house. When you are driving around or have stopped in traffic somebody may be interested enough to record your phone number. This method has the added advantage that the person has already seen the car and noted its condition before he phones you (but also the way in which you drive it!). You can buy, for about £8, a complete DIY car sale kit, which includes a display card with peel-and-stick numbers and words to make up your FOR SALE message. If you are displaying your car in a busy street this could save you pounds in advertising and, of course, you can always use the kit again.

Pre-paid Adverts in Newspapers and Magazines

Newspapers and magazines usually charge for each word used, so it is important to keep such adverts brief and to the point. However, take care not to use hopelessly and unnecessarily abbreviated words that the reader may not understand. It *won't* actually save you money. Check that all the necessary information is included: in one advert I saw recently the seller forgot to name the model. He advertised a Ford Estate; which one, Sierra, Cortina, Granada, Escort?! I would guess that with the volume and variety of other adverts in that paper he did not get much response.

Consider the following three adverts for a Vauxhall Senator 3.0-litre CDi model registered in 1985; finished in champagne gold with matching interior trim; slight collision damage; ten months' MOT and two months' road tax.

Figure 21 *Vauxhall Senator advertisements for comparison*

1.
> **Senator. B-reg.** Good condition, 3 owners, reliable car. All extras, tax, MOT. Smart looker. £1,700. (0684) 005002.

2.
> **Senator 3.0i CD,** 1985, gold with matching interior, 4-speed auto, 56,000 miles; recent front tyres and brake discs; rust protected; much history; long MOT; taxed December. Alarmed, stereo/cassette; clean, reliable prestige car (small dent in passenger door).
>
> £1,695 o.n.o. Charles (0684) 005089/90684) 005194 (eves).

3.
> **1985 Vauxhall** Senator, B-reg, no rust, radio/cassette, MOT, tax, s/r, c/l, r.h.w, e/m, f.s.h, new parts, ex. con/immac. inside and out. Average mileage. Drives perfect. First to see will buy, p/x poss. £1,700. (0684) 005291.

Which one would you follow up if interested? Let's examine ad 1: it is brief and punchy, which is good, but many of the words are wasted. For example, the seller need not have pointed out at this stage that you are about to become the car's fourth owner – this is *not* a selling-point. He has neglected to tell you the colour of the car, which is important to many buyers. B-registration can mean either 1984 or 1985 and he would have done better in this case to have said 1985 (if the car had been a 1984 B-reg, he should have left it as it is, to suggest that the car could be younger, that is, 1985). He has hinted at 'extras' but does not disclose what they are – for instance, does he mean four-speed automatic gearbox, fog-lamps and air-conditioning, or fluffy dice, spare keys and stickers? The car has been taxed and carries an MOT but for how long – until next week? It does not give even the most basic information and so the buyer does not really know what is being sold. This advert would have cost about £8 in a local paper and is unlikely to sell first time. It is a poor advert but typical of many you will see in the papers. (See also figures 22a and 22b).

Now look at ad 3. The message here is mixed and confusing; the abbreviations are meaningless to the layman. Some of the claims are difficult to believe (for example, no rust on a car that is nine years old!). The colour of the car has been omitted, and radio/cassette players are relatively low-value items that need not be mentioned at this stage. The tone is brash and overconfident ('First to see will buy'), and the offer of a part-exchange ('p/x') tells you nothing useful about the car except that the seller could be a dealer.

Also most people looking to buy a Senator would know already that Vauxhall make them, so listing just the model would've been adequate. It would have been helpful too to know exactly what was meant by 'average mileage' – could it mean *average* for a 30,000-mile-a-year rep? Finally, if the car drives *so* well, why is the owner selling?

In ad 2 the seller has started by clarifying the age, colour, engine size and trim level of the model, thus eliminating the guesswork for the buyer. The descriptions do not exaggerate ('clean', not 'immaculate'), and this suggests integrity in the seller. 'Long MOT' should mean at least nine months left, and we are told when the tax disc expires. He has also made himself available to speak to potential buyers at all times. This advert should attract a big response; try to write a similar one, briefly disclosing all relevant and attractive points.

It is probably advisable to include 'o.n.o.' (or nearest offer) to give a little scope for negotiation. All potential customers like to feel they can bargain with you to some extent; you could add a little to the asking price to allow for this. Do not invite offers without naming an asking price – it makes the customer's task too difficult.

Do bear in mind that adverts for cars are usually listed alphabetically beginning with the make or model names; for example, Volvo, Renault, Escort, etc., and an advert written 'B-reg Volvo 240, etc.' is likely to become buried in the adverts for cars listed under B. Therefore, always begin your advert with the appropriate make or model.

The following are genuine advertisements taken from a southern newspaper during 1993. They are the kind of advert you should try to avoid writing.

Focusses on all the secondary items, for example, 'cartel body kit', 'pull out stereo', 'special wheels', leaving little doubt as to how the car is likely to have been driven. Car has also become a money pit ('maintained regardless of cost'), and ad omits the more important items such as: service history, length of MOT and tax, number of owners and even colour.

These tell you nothing very useful about the cars. For example, they could have mentioned colour, recent new parts, seat fabric, spec extras and/or accessories, in fact anything that could create a better picture of the model (note: the Volvo ad doesn't even tell us the model!).

An ad that really says everything bad about the car: 'super driver', 'radio', 'super bargain' – all typical of small-time dealer slang. What about some service history, (long) MOT, and tax (which is a dealer's responsibility, after all)? This could turn out to be one of the most expensive cars you could buy.

This ad wastes too many words – for example, an Escort is obviously a Ford, and the month of manufacture gives away that this is a very early G-plater as opposed to a later 1990 model. Even 'immac' condition is hard to believe on anything but a brand-new model. Notice the lack of MOT, service history, colour or even trim level (L,GL). This ad could have started better: 'ESCORT 1.8D G-reg...'

Figure 22a *The type of advertisement to avoid writing*

Figure 22b *Examples of better advertisements*

Extras

A word about any extras you might include. If there is anything that you do not want to sell then make sure you do not advertise it at the outset (in fact remove it from the car). Only advertise a radio/cassette, for example, if it is in working order; if it is not, leave it there but do not advertise it. The same applies to other items and accessories such as tax discs, mats, rugs, roof-racks, dog-guards or headrests. You have to make clear what is and what is not for sale to avoid disputes later. A point you might remember is that if you've just bought an altogether different model you will probably no longer require things like your old handbook, roof-rack, spare spark-plugs, points, colour-restorer pen, etc. It can be useful at negotiating time to offer to throw these items in, in order to hold your asking price.

Final Figure

■■■ HOT TIP ■■■■■■■■■■■■

In determining your selling price, avoid rounding the figure since it appears to leave the customer no room for negotiation. For instance, if you are selling your 1987 Citroën BX 14E for £2,000, you are actually less likely to get a response to your advert than if you asked for £1,995. A difference of only £5 to you, but to the customer it may seem an invitation to negotiate down to £1,900, possibly more than you thought you would get anyway. You do not see figure rounding on dealers' forecourts for this very reason.

Truth in Advertising

This point will be covered more thoroughly in 10.9, but remember that your advert must be accurate. Coaxing a person into thinking that a car is faster or more popular than he had believed is one thing, but outright lying about any aspect of the car, such as a reconditioned engine or recent service when it has had neither, is illegal.

10.5 Preparations for Selling – How to Present Your Car

Having described, valued and priced your car for advertisement it makes sense to present it in the best condition possible for when potential buyers come to visit. This does take a bit of work, especially if the car has mechanical and/or structural defects. But good preparation for sale can make a substantial difference to the selling price. Many people do not bother to prepare their cars adequately, so this is another reason, especially if yours is a popular model, to give it an even better chance of competing.

Structural and Mechanical Defects

If your car has serious defects you will have to decide if it will be worth spending much on it at all.

Even if you do not have a current MOT certificate, this need not deter you from trying to sell from a newspaper advert. Remember that there is a share of the market willing to buy cars with faults – people do work on them for a hobby. To sell legally, of course, you must declare any major faults; for example, fuel-injection trouble, defective steering or brakes, serious oil leaks and so on. You can be honest without giving a catalogue of faults by saying 'good condition for the year' – if this is true. Your customer may know where to get parts cheaply and if this is the case you need not drop your asking price by very much. The same applies to structural and bodywork blemishes including dented or badly rusted body panels and sills. Even if you do not attempt to repair the parts yourself, you ought to get some idea of the cost of their replacement.

Appearance

The biggest single factor governing whether your asking price will be met can be reduced to the superficial – that is, the car's overall appearance. You will, no doubt, already know how important and interchangeable the ideas of car and image are. Cars are chosen as special possessions that speak volumes about a person, and are symbols with which many people identify. Therefore you can expect that a potential buyer, already excited by your advert, will be even more pleased if the car looks 'the business', and will almost certainly be willing to accept its few faults, without killing the asking price.

For best results, prepare your car in the following way:

Washing

- Rinse or hose with cold water to loosen surface dirt
- Properly wash with a car shampoo, soaping every nook and cranny that is capable of retaining dirt, including the bumpers, valance, radiator grille, windscreen wipers, wing mirrors and wheel arch folds. Start washing at the top of the car and work down to the lower panels. Pay attention to wheels and tyres, using one sponge for soapy water and another to rinse. Dry with a chamois-leather – even artificial ones are quite effective – or use a large clean dustsheet
- Apply a wax polish (Turtle or Simoniz brands are good) or a product called Autoglym
- As an alternative to the previous suggestion, and if the bodywork is still showing signs of ingrained dirt, use a colour restorer. T-cut is one of the most popular. It works by taking off a tiny fraction of paint as you buff it in (and so is capable of removing very superficial scratches and rust), leaving a shining showroom finish. You can buy T-cut for metallic and solid colours alike.

Windows

Windows account for somewhere between one fifth and a quarter of the bodywork and so bright, gleaming glass will do wonders for a buyer's confidence in you as a previous owner.

- Wash the glass with soapy water, rinse off and dry with a cloth, chamois or dust-sheet
- Apply Sainsbury's Clean & Bright Glass Cleaner, buffing in with a clean dry cloth or tissue. Repeat this step for all windows both inside and out
- Remove any old stickers that may offend a potential buyer (MY OTHER CAR'S A LOTUS, for example). You can remove marks made by old stickers with a dab of white spirit on the glass followed by immediate washing with water.

Interiors

A well-kept interior should not need much attention. However, let's assume the worst scenario: that you have *never* cleaned the car out:

- Take out all removable carpets and mats and scrub off any dried-on-dirt with a stiff brush. Deep-seated dirt will surface and can be removed with a vacuum cleaner after this. Scrub any non-removable fabrics in like fashion with an appropriate brush
- Hoover carpets and mats with a wide vacuum attachment
- With a narrow attachment vacuum the ceiling/head-lining fabric and search all the boundaries for grime – it if got here in the first place, it can be removed. Take out the spare wheel(s) and any tools from the boot area and dredge up all the dirt from the corners
- Use a damp cloth for any plastic or metal parts that are dirty and either vacuum or scrub with detergent (as appropriate) the inner door trim fabric. Use strong glue to stick back any of this material that has peeled away since peeling door fabric can only show neglect on the driver's part

● When cleaning the dashboard/facia, steering-wheel and controls you can use a spray-on or wipe-on polish (such as Carisma), which can bring out a remarkable finish. Be careful not to inhale these sprays since many are toxic.

Dogs

● If you have carried dogs in the back, it is possible that shed hairs will be difficult to shift – even with a vacuum cleaner – and will have to be painstakingly picked up with a damp cloth
● Teeth marks are not so easy to deal with but any torn or split upholstery or carpet can at least be sewn back together or glued down again
● Lingering dog smells are best dealt with by using air fresheners. The best type are the suspended ones, like the Feu Orange range, rather than the type you affix to a surface in the car, which sometimes leave a mark when removed.

Smoke Stains

● Remember to empty the ashtrays. Make sure these are absolutely clean since to a non-smoker there is nothing worse than taking over a car previously driven by someone who smoked habitually
● Smoke-stained ceilings are difficult to disguise but one remedy is to use a dilute shampoo solution (applied with a brush) to the headlining fabric (as long as the material can suitably take this) and then remove with a clean cloth. Fruit- and herbal-based shampoos are the best and, as well as reducing the staining, they leave an altogether more pleasant odour.

Under-bonnet Preparation

Anything that will make an engine look clean (and hence appear better looked after) will improve your chances of selling.

- I repeat the advantage of a steam clean (it will also pinpoint the source of any leaks); and for as little as £15 this is arguably better and less messy than applying and then removing a degreasant yourself. However, as the steam clean is more for the benefit of the buyer than the seller, I would advise that unless the engine bay is very dirty you do not waste unnecessary time and money
- Ensure that the bonnet underside itself is clean and free from rusty water stains, in particular
- Also, remove any leaves trapped in the air-ventilation inlets and radiator fins/grille, if visible.

Hoses, Fan Belts, Battery, Radiator and Fluid Levels

- While the bonnet is up, look for cracking or fraying fan belts or bulging radiator hoses – if so, you can at least offer your spares as replacements
- Wipe off any water stains on the hoses
- Clean the battery terminals of caked-on or powdery deposits and then coat them generously with Vaseline or petroleum jelly
- Also, clear any white battery sludge that has accumulated in the battery tray; check that the battery is secure and not likely to move around when the car is in motion; that the case is clean; and that there is sufficient distilled water to cover the plates of each cell. The charge should be good. (You can put it on trickle charge for a couple of hours if it is low)

- Top up the radiator level if low, and clean the radiator cap if dirty or rust-coloured inside. If you know of a radiator leak then use a temporary Radweld-type sealant (£2–£3), which can fix it in minutes
- Always assume that the buyer is going to check these points, as well as all fluid levels, so make sure there is sufficient oil on the dipstick. Look also at the (automatic) gearbox fluid level, the brake fluid level, and check that the windscreen washer bottles are topped up.

▆▆▆ HOT TIP ▆▆▆

The buyer may not even try the windscreen wipers, but if even one is seriously frayed, replace it. You stand a much better chance of retaining your, possibly high, asking price if you can demonstrate that all such details are in good working order.

Rusted Paintwork and Small Scratches

Overall clean and tidy appearance will do much to overshadow minor blemishes. When rusting has developed from a scratch you will have to decide whether to leave it alone or to cover it.

- Light, superficial rust can be gently sanded off with emery cloth, steel wool or an aluminium oxide strip – take care not to scratch local and otherwise intact paintwork
- When down to the metal apply even-layered strokes with a paint touch-up stick. It can be very difficult to match the touch-up paint exactly with the original colour, especially if it is a metallic finish, but even if

it is detectable the prospective buyer will see that you have at least cared enough to disguise the scratch in the first place

● Repeat this procedure for stone-chip marks if present on the valance, grille and bonnet areas.

Steel Wheels, Chrome and Other Brightwork

● If the shining finish to the brightwork (metal window frames, door handles, bumper trim, etc.) and wheels has dulled, remove visible rust with wire wool or a stiff wire brush and get down to a smooth finish

● Apply a chrome cleaner to bring out a shine. There are quite a few handy all-round products claiming to do more than one job. There is a Wheel Cleaner kit, which does both alloy and steel wheels, and Simoniz Black Diamond car valeting kit which will do black plastics, rubber and also vinyl hoods.

Alloy Wheels

Kerbing and brake dust corrosion will have left an unsightly powdery deposit on the wheels where the lacquer (which protects against corrosion) has been taken off.

● Sanding down with fine abrasive paper and re-lacquering will bring them up again

● The Wheel Cleaner kit mentioned above will do the same.

Tyres

Kerbing and country lane driving will have scraped, muddied and chalked the tyres.

● Wash as necessary and scrub with a brush, at the same time removing any stones or glass, etc., from the tyre grooves and drainage channels

● Apply Armor All's Protectant or Tyre Foam. For best results apply this a few days *before* selling to let the newness fade a little. Properly applied, there should be sufficient to do all four wheels many times over.

Registration Number-plates

If the number-plate is broken, or if any of the digits are obscured, buy a new once since this is now an MOT test item. You can buy a single front or rear reflective acrylic-type plate for as little as £7, which can be done while you wait – you will need to bring your registration certificate as proof of ownership.

There is no end to the list of possible pre-sale preparations you could attempt on your car, but it is only within the scope of this book to deal with some of the more cosmetic ones. You can find other tips and remedies in the good weekly and monthly DIY motoring magazines. Remember that a buyer coming to view your car should instantly receive a good impression of it. He should anticipate at least some imperfections, however, which will no doubt be reflected in your asking price. No-one should be expecting to be sold a *new* car. You are applying the above preparative treatments simply to give yourself the greatest chance of securing the best possible price.

Professional Valeting

If, however, you don't already have many of the above-mentioned products, and are unwilling to spend the time valeting your own car, you can always have it done by a professional company. This can take anywhere between three and seven hours depending on the size of car and kind of service you want, and can cost up to

£100 for the full valet (interior, exterior, steam clean, wash, wax, polish, etc.). If you do elect for a valeting company to do the job you will find best value in letting them do it all.

10.6 How to Deal with Buyers

On the Phone

Your first task is to turn that initial inquiry into a definite appointment. This is much easier said than done, however, and it is often a good start to indicate to the buyer that he is only one of many interested parties. Don't confirm excitedly that, 'The car is still for sale . . . it is in truly excellent condition . . . only one owner . . . great bodywork . . . MOT'd . . . a fabulous bargain . . .' – selling a car is a two-way process and people really don't want high-pressure sales talk but would prefer to have found themselves a bargain by their own shrewdness, good luck and initiative. Try to let the buyer ask his questions in his own time.

HOT TIP

When it comes to arranging a time to view the car, fix an exact appointment. When people say they will come round 'some time tomorrow', they will feel less obliged to you than if they have arranged to meet you at a specified time.

Vehicle Inspections

If your buyer asks if he can bring a vehicle inspector (either from the AA or privately), and you have nothing to hide, then it is best to agree. The very fact that you appear to welcome an inspection can often be the reassurance the buyer was looking for and he may be happy to forget the expense of using an inspector after all. However, it has been known for some private inspectors to overstate the defects in a car, and even to become aggressive with the seller! Almost certainly you can expect that a consequence of the vehicle inspection will be a drop in your asking price. If you do not want an independent assessor to visit then say so – give the reason that you know the inspection will take two to three hours (and then a further day or two for the report to be finished) and that you have already had two keen customers on the phone, who you wouldn't want to lose. If this deters the customer then so be it; there should be another along soon. Incidentally, you should question the motives of someone who insists on a professional vehicle inspection if the car you are selling is fairly old and under about £500 (despite the fact that this is precisely the price range of car that could need it most).

At Your House

When the buyer arrives, and especially if you haven't had much experience in selling cars, remember that all you are doing is selling a car to someone you have never met previously and will probably never see again. It is not a supreme test of wills to see who'll back down first. Expect the buyer to be critical and to ask many pointed questions and then to try to knock down your asking price. Let him take his time in looking around the car and try not to give the impression that you are watching him like a hawk. If there is someone with him, chat to him or her about something altogether different: where they live, how far they have had to travel, etc. Smile, be friendly and remember that a worried or anxious expression (coupled with mumbled replies) can be enough to lose you the sale. Desperation to sell always shows, whatever the product, and is off-putting.

Defects

If the car has a potentially serious fault you should admit it (after all, you would want to be treated in the same way), and if it is a glaring fault you should have advertised it already, bearing in mind your legal responsibilities as a private seller (see 10.9).

When showing him the car, accentuate the positive and, whatever car you are selling, remark that you didn't realize just how sought-after these models were – especially those in good condition. This is not high-pressure salesmanship, more persuading the customer that he probably won't get such a good deal elsewhere and that he might regret it if he doesn't buy this one. If there is visible damage to the wheels, bodywork, bumper, lights, etc., then be honest about what happened and if you have not remedied it yourself, suggest how he could go about it. But don't lie about the cost of repairs – if things are *that* cheap or easy to fix then why have you not done them yourself?

There is no set routine to selling a car – some buyers will prefer to examine structurally and mechanically to their satisfaction, while others will not even bother with a test drive if they like what they see; some don't know what they are looking for, yet will want to look as though they do; and others, still, will be happy for *you* to give them all the information. In the latter case try to keep things moving by showing them the driver's seat and encouraging them to test-drive. It will help to have the engine already warm in order that it starts first time. Naturally, you will be familiar with the behaviour of your car and if first-time starting can be temperamental you should offer the keys to the buyer to start it. If he fails first time, then offer to do it yourself: as long as the car *will* start, you will give a better impression if you can demonstrate its operation with ease.

◼ HOT TIP ◼

Go with the customer on the test-drive no matter how plausible his reason for wanting to drive on his own, and remember only to let him drive if he can demonstrate adequate insurance cover, otherwise you drive (in fact this is arranged on the phone beforehand).

Finally, be quick to respond to any questions, especially ones concerning the handling and temperament of the car: remember again, the truth – glossing over reasons for light tapping noises on start-up is one thing, but outright lying to achieve a sale is not on.

Reasons for Sale

The best reasons are always genuine and often apparent: for example, you have acquired a lease car for your work; you need something bigger or smaller or more economical (not the best reason to state); you habitually change your car after so many years, etc. But whatever the reason make it sound sensible – have you, yourself, ever come away disappointed from what *seemed* like an otherwise nice enough car, but didn't buy because there was something about the seller, or what he said, that you didn't like or trust?

After the test drive, the buyer might want to have another look under the bonnet in order to confirm or allay any problems he suspected earlier: take this as a second chance to highlight the good points – fan belt replacements, new spark-plugs, air and oil filters, renewed radiator hoses, etc.

Most buyers will inquire about reliability and, today, most cars are reliable – if properly serviced and maintained. When replying, it is more reassuring for the buyer to hear that a car has done a higher than average mileage through regular, daily distance driving than that it has a low mileage from being driven twice a week for the two-minute drive to Tesco. The latter will most definitely be storing up serious problems (see 2.2).

If all is going well with the customer so far, you will be keen to finalize the sale. Remember to mention those useful extras – roof-rack, handbook, paint touch-up stick, etc.

HOT TIP

Above all (and especially if there is more than one person present), be particularly careful about making any kind of promise or guarantee about the car that you know you cannot honour. It is a responsibility you do not need or have to provide and, even more importantly, be clear about anything you put into writing.

10.7 Paperwork

It helps to have all the documents ready: first, the vehicle registration certificate – the familiar blue-and-pink or blue-and-white DVLA form that will probably show your name as the official owner of the car. On selling the car you tear off the bottom strip and record in that portion the name and address of the buyer, the date of selling, and the current mileage, sign it and mail to the DVLC as soon as possible (see 9.1 for address). It is important to do this immediately since, if you delay, you could be made responsible for certain future abuses of the car, including speeding and parking fines, which would find their way to you if the DVLC had not been notified of a change of ownership. I know people who have had to take considerable time off work to try to prove they were not responsible for such fines, and who, at the end of the day, have still been made to pay for them.

The other main document is the MOT certificate, which any car over three years old must have to demonstrate its roadworthiness. If you do not have a current MOT see 10.9 for what to do. If you've had the car from new or bought it from a far-sighted owner, you should have all the relevant MOT, service history and maintenance records. Although it is not essential to have them all, psychologically it reassures the buyer that the car has enjoyed good previous ownership. You do not have to show the original bill of sale unless challenged, but it is a good idea to have it available as extra evidence that the car *is* yours to sell.

10.8 Money

When you have agreed your final price, safeguard against fraud by insisting on cash. Most people do come prepared to pay in cash since they know this is often the only way they will be able to take the car away the same day. At the very least you should insist on a cash deposit with a simple written agreement drawn up to hold the car over for a certain number of days until the balance is cleared. The only other sensible alternative is to accept a banker's draft, which in principle is worth cash. To some extent it depends on who it is you are dealing with, but you would be advised to avoid personal cheques; if you do take one, explain that since a cheque guarantee card will honour up to £50 only the buyer will have to wait three to four days for the cheque to clear before taking the car away – a useful way to remind him that he *can* find the cash after all!

If a cheque bounces and, even worse, no address is recorded (and this does happen!) this further reduces your chances of getting either the money back *or* your car returned.

Preparing a Bill of Sale

Have prepared a bill of sale on the following lines, typed in advance if you can:
NOTE: If you do accept a deposit, write a separate receipt for that and retain the bill of sale until the balance is settled in full.

10.9 Selling a Car with Defects – Your Legal Responsibilities

Whether you are a dealer or private seller you must realize that to sell a vehicle with certain defects is a criminal offence despite the fact that you might have been ignorant of them. Such defects (as covered by the Road Traffic Act) include steering, brakes, tyres, compulsory lights and reflectors. In the latter cases, claiming that you didn't know the buyer intended to use the car

Your Address

Tel:

Sold, 1 Mk IV Cortina 2.3GL Estate
Reg. No: CJN 683T (1979)
Colour: Blue
VIN/
CHASSIS: XXXWFOXX224GAFXX
Recorded Mileage: 102,326 miles
Sold as seen and approved at the price
of £525

To: Mr?Mrs?Miss C.A.R. Hunter on 10/8/92

of (Address)

Signature

Deposit paid £200 cash 10/8/92
Balance to be cleared in 5 days.

Signature

Figure 23 *Preparing a bill of sale*

after dark is not much protection and, while it is the responsibility of the buyer to check these items himself, he could argue to the contrary afterwards. What you need to do is to eliminate any comebacks on a car you sell by knowing the law as it applies to you. There are very few rules that bind you, as we have seen, but it is important for you to know them just in case the buyer does too.

If you are really not sure if the vehicle you are selling is roadsafe you can sell it as a non-runner, although the chances of your realizing the best price on a car described in this way are rather unlikely. What you can do is sell the car as it is now with *written* notice of any defects that will have to be serviced prior to the buyer's use of it. Whether or not the buyer makes good the repairs is not your concern since, if need be, you could then produce a photocopy of that notice as proof. Many people assume a car with a current MOT certificate to be perfectly roadworthy and legal to drive; however, serious defects could have occurred since the MOT test date, rendering the vehicle both dangerous and illegal. Prosecutions against private sellers are usually very few and far between, mainly because of ignorance on the part of the buyer, who may not fully realize his rights. This does not mean, though, that you have an open licence to sell any car below roadworthy standard.

Guarantees

As a private seller, all you need guarantee is that your sales talk is accurate and that you are not actually misleading the buyer about any new, reconditioned or second-hand parts that might have been fitted. You must not dupe a potential buyer into thinking he is getting, for instance, a new battery when in fact this was purchased over a year ago; this can make you liable if the seller has proof that you said this in your advert and wants to pursue the matter. However, if you clock the mileage and declare the true amount of this in writing, or that you know this has been done, then you are selling quite within the law.

A buyer cannot claim from you if he believes that he paid too much for the vehicle since neither you nor anybody else actually forced him to buy it. The car does not have to be worth the price and neither do you have to sell it fit for use – points often not appreciated by the buyer. If the car develops a fault even the very next day, and you made no promises about the offending component(s), then, technically, you are within the law. On moral grounds, though, you might see fit to offer some financial remedy, as a gesture.

One thing in your favour is that the longer a buyer takes before he returns to complain (and he might think he can complain about anything), the weaker his case is since you can argue that any such fault developed while the vehicle was in his possession, or that a significant delay in his return indicates that he was happy to accept the car with its fault (that is, sold as seen and approved).

In practice, it may be better to suggest arranging an independent inspection of the vehicle (at the buyer's expense), and then pointing out that he'd have to pursue the matter through a small claims (or other) court, with no guarantee of winning. This might be deterrent enough and he may be more willing to pay for the replacement part(s) himself.

AUTO-CHECK
Vehicle Inspections

DISCLAIMER

What you are buying in a used car is 'unused miles' or the useful life left in it by the previous owner(s). Conducting a vehicle inspection can by no means guarantee a good-as-new or bargain car, or even that you're looking at reasonable value.

A (used) car contains many thousands of components – any number of which may be in a poor state of wear or about to default and so the purpose of the inspection will be to try to determine the car's present condition and to warn of anything serious that is about to malfunction either now or in the very near future and, therefore, to help minimize the risk of buying bad.

With any second-hand car you must expect to have to spend some money in order to restore it to a reasonable level, and this will depend largely on the vehicle's age, present condition and, of course, you.

A vehicle inspector will provide an opinion of the car's structural and mechanical merits and will, to the best of his ability, advise on matters relating to likely previous ownership and service history and will try to protect you under any relevant areas of the Sale of Goods Act. The inspector can estimate what he believes the car to be worth. He cannot, however, be accountable for any errors, omissions, misleading statements or advice which later turn out to be incorrect.

You are under no obligation to buy and, at the end of the day, it will be solely your decision whether or not to purchase a particular vehicle. It is on this basis that the inspection is conducted. Thank you for choosing Auto-Check Vehicle Inspections.

Signature _____ Date _____

Figure 24a *Vehicle pre-inspection disclaimer*

Checklists

Overleaf is a near-exhaustive checklist comprising many of the items you could expect to examine in the time available. Bear in mind, too, that not all makes of car are equipped to the same extent and so some components and functions may well be excluded from the list, such as sun-roof, air-conditioning, fog-lamps, anti-roll bars, prop shafts, etc.

Remember also that there are both good and bad reasons to reject a car. A seriously worn engine or balking gearbox, defective steering or vast areas of the bodywork that have been hastily filled with plastic padding are usually good reasons to pass up a particular example, especially if these defects are collective. Thumbnail scratches or dents in the coachwork, scruffy-looking interior, a resprayed body panel or engine misfire, on the other hand, can each be fairly easily or cheaply remedied if not altogether tolerated. Above all, try to think in terms of the likely costs of repair before making a snap decision.

	Pass	Fail	Comments
Visual Inspection			
overall appearance			
panel lesions/misaligned coachlines			
doors (rust, filler, etc.)			
bonnet			
boot tailgate			
lower panels			
roof/roof-rack/guttering			
wheel arches			
door sills/inner sills			
front/rear bumpers			
valance, grille			
light cluster lenses			
pillars (A, B, C, D posts)			
respray			
repaired/replacement panels			
bodywork badges			
exhaust backbox and downpipes			
tailpipe colour			
exhaust bracket security			
towbar and electrics			
petrol/fuel tank (leaks)			
petrol cap/flap			
brake pipes			
jacking points			
tyres (spec., size, wear)			
wheel rim condition			
dust caps, lug-nuts			
spare wheel			
wheel bearings			
windscreens (stickers, cracks)			
windscreen rubber condition			
wiper blades			
security window etching			
tax disc validity			
number-plates (condition)			
wing mirrors (condition)			
general suspension (sags, bounce test)			

Figure 24b *Structural, mechanical, electrical and road tests*

	Pass	Fail	Comments
Underside			
chassis rails			
floorings			
prop shaft (not front-wheel drive)			
drive shafts (play, gaiters)			
shock absorbers (leaks)			
brake pipes and hoses			
coil springs			
leaf springs			
suspension mountings rear axle (leaks, rust)			
anti-roll bar mounts			
oil filter (condition)			
ball joints/track rod ends			
steering arms			
steering rack gaiters			
engine oil puddles			
gearbox oil puddles			
water puddles			
Interior			
general impression			
mileage feasibility			
seats (sags, rips)			
seat-belts			
pedal rubbers			
water leaks (carpets, boot, stains, misted windows)			
carpets/mats			
headlining			
dashboard			
interior curtesy/warning lights			
ignition lock			
stereo/cassette			
dog grille/animal hairs			
velour, leather (wear)			
door trim			
slack switchgear/door handles			
window winders			

	Pass	Fail	Comments
Interior continued			
central locking			
sun-roof/windows			
horn			
sidelights			
headlights			
main beam			
indicators/hazards			
reflectors			
reversing/driving/fog-lights			
Engine Bay			
engine appearance/bonnet underside			
inner panels/suspension mountings			
battery and tray			
air filter			
fan belts			
HT (ignition) leads			
distributor cap			
coil connection			
rotor arm			
spark-plug tips			
coolant level/colour			
radiator			
fan water pump (condition, play)			
brake master cylinder (leaks, rust)			
brake fluid level			
brake servo unit			
fuel lines			
oil filler cap			
dipstick oil level/condition			
automatic gearbox oil level			
radiator hoses			
power steering fluid level/colour			
VIN plate (condition)			

	Pass	Fail	Comments
Mechanical Tests			
starting ability			
ignition/oil warning lights			
exhaust emission colour			
exhaust emission on hard revs			
tailpipe vibration (leaks)			
idling noise (smooth, lumpy)			
cam shaft rattle (persistent)			
flat spots			
compression test (each cylinder)			
clutch			
gearbox (selection)			
brake servo unit			
handbrake			
parking brake (automatic gearbox only)			
steering			
power steering			
battery (visual inspection and drop test)			
Road Test			
comfort/vibrations			
brake effectiveness			
acceleration			
wheel bearings			
steering response/noise			
steering column switchgear			
windscreen washer/wipers			
suspension			
gearbox selection/precision			
exhaust fumes/noise			
dashboard instruments			
aerial			
axle/differential noises			
turbo (boost pressure, smoke, whistling, clatter)			
four-wheel drive (low-range gear selection			
air ventilation/heating			

	Pass	Fail	Comments
Do the Following Relate to the Vehicle Registration Certificate (V5)?			
front/rear number-plates			
name and address of vendor			
VIN plate(s)			
bodywork colour			
bodywork style (saloon, coupé, etc.)			
engine size (1500cc, 2.0 litres, etc.)			
specification (GL, LX, SE, etc.)			
type of fuel (diesel or petrol)			
transmission (automatic, manual)			
age of car			
present vendor's length of ownership			
private car/former taxi or other			
Service History			
is service booklet complete?			
is each mileage interval clearly stamped?			
are all repair/service bills included?			
MOT Certificates			
are there several old MOT papers present or just the current certificate?			
Questions to Ask the Owner			
anything major wrong with the car?			
what were its main uses and journeys?			
any special starting procedure?			
any outstanding finance payments? (get in writing)			
do you have the original bill of sale?			
any quirks about the car's handling, etc., that I should know about?			
any transferable warrannties that are unexpired to date?			
any other accessories (bulbs, fan belts, etc.) to throw in?			
main reason for selling the car?			
does it run on leaded or unleaded (if petrol)?			

Auto-Check Vehicle Inspections © 1991

Figure 24c *Documentation and service history checklist*

Summary

Below is a five-point plan to help you buy a better used car. Be sure to consider all criteria.

- **Buy Genuine:** take the necessary time and precautions to weed out undesirable cars, including stolen, poorly rebuilt vehicles following crash damage or those that have been customized; for example, over-tuned engines, dropped suspensions, body kits etc.
- **Buy Clean:** try to buy a car that has had as few owners from new as possible, with the V5 clearly in the seller's name; purchase *at* their address; cross-check VIN numbers with the V5; ensure as much service history as possible (which needn't necessarily be from a main dealer) and with a long MOT certificate (if applicable)
- **Buy for a Fair Price:** research at least the ballpark price for the car *before* you buy. Study used-car price guides, dealer forecourts and also newspaper adverts for similar models. Buy when the car's depreciation period is levelling off (at roughly three years)
- **Know Your Model:** research a prospective model's track record, recall history, faults and shortcomings, running costs, including insurance, fuel consumption, ease of servicing/maintenance, and both price and availability of spares. Stop and speak to owners of like models for any valuable information *before* you buy
- **Consider Resale Value:** by all means choose your dream car, but spare a thought for the future. Choose colour, engine size and specification with care and, in particular, a car with a proven popularity.

Bibliography

The Motorist and the Law: A Guide to Motorists' Rights, John Pritchard (Penguin Books, 1987).

AA Car Care (AA Publishing, 1986).

Haynes Ford Granada Owners' Workshop Manual 481 (Haynes Publishing Group, 1986).

The Motorists' Price Guide (Foxpride)

Parker's Used, New & Trade Car Price Guide (Parker Mead)

Haynes Owners' Workshop Manual (specific model)

How to Get More Miles Per Gallon, Sikorsky and Rowlands (Arrow Books, 1980).

Index